The First and Second Books of Adam and Eve

The Conflict With Satan

Edited by Joseph Lumpkin

Joseph B. Lumpkin

The First and Second Books of Adam and Eve
The Conflict With Satan

Copyright © 2009 Joseph Lumpkin

All rights reserved.

Fifth Estate Publishers,

Post Office Box 116, Blountsville, AL 35031.

First Printing 2009

Cover by An Quigley

Printed on acid-free paper

Library of Congress Control No: 2009901054

ISBN: 978-1-933580-52-4

1-933580-52-6

Fifth Estate

2009

Joseph B. Lumpkin

The First Book of Adam and Eve
The Conflict With Satan

The First Book of Adam and Eve is an apocryphal story, written in a midrash style, detailing the life of Adam and Eve from the time God planted the Garden of Eden to the time that Cain killed his brother, Abel.

The story is a fanciful embellishment of the Genesis story up to the point of the cursing of Cain for the murder of Abel.

Of the numerous apocryphal works that were written regarding Adam and Eve this text seems to have most influenced early theologians. This is evident in the widespread popularity of the book from the third to the thirteenth century. Even though the book was widely read in the Middle Ages, and considered to shine light on what actually took place in the time of creation, today it is considered fiction and thus relegated to a collection of texts called the Pseudepigrapha, or "false writings."

The text shows some cobbling together of various works, combined into a single storyline. Although the foundation of the text can be traced to combined oral traditions thousands of years old, the primary story was likely created around two or three hundred years before Christ. Additions and details were added over many years, leading to this version being penned around the 3rd century A.D.

The text presented here is an embellishment of the Jewish storyline from Genesis that is "Christianized" by additions of allusions and references to the New Testament. Quite often the details of the story are made to foreshadow the birth, death, and resurrection of Jesus. The result is the text before you.

The central part of the text focuses on the conflict between Good and Evil in the form of Satan's endeavor to destroy God's creations, Adam and Eve. The story begs the eternal question, how does one know whether God or Satan guides the opportunity, situation, or person confronting us. The fight between good and evil, as well as the question of who is influencing our surroundings, are eternal, and the story attempts to answer in metaphor.

The creation story and the tale of Adam and Eve pervaded the thoughts of writers throughout the ancient world. Evidence is seen in the large number of versions that exist in various languages and cultures. Indeed, it is due to the amazing popularity of the text that it has survived in six languages: Greek, Latin, Armenian, Georgian, and Slavonic, as well as a fragment in Coptic. The stories may also be traced through the writings of Greeks, Syrians, Egyptians, Abyssinians, Hebrews, and other ancient peoples.

Most scholars agree that the text was written originally in Greek and that all of the six versions show evidence of Greek linguistic roots. Those Greek manuscripts we posses seem to be no more accurate to the original than any of the other translations, having been so many generations removed from the source document.

The foundation of our modern English translation began with

the work of, Vicar of Broadwindsor, Dr. S. C. Malan, who worked from the Ethiopic edition edited by, Professor at the University of Munich. Dr. Trumpp, who had the advantage of having an older version at his disposal.

From an ancient oral tradition, to a 3rd century codex, through the hands of Dr. E. Trumpp and Dr. S. C. Malan, to this modern English version, the First Book of Adam and Eve has survived, just as mankind has survived the struggles written of in the book itself.

The Malan translation of the text was penned in a rather stilted and formal style of English resembling that of the King James Bible. The Malan translation was then taken and re-written with word choices and sentence structure altered to make it more palatable and understandable to the modern reader, while keeping the poetic flow of the text.

Notes and references are added in italicized font. Alternate words or phrases that may add more depth or possibilities in translation are place in parentheses.

The First Book of Adam and Eve

Chapter I

1 On the third day, God planted the garden in the east of the earth, on the border of the world in the eastward direction toward and beyond the rising sun. There one finds nothing but water that encompasses the whole world and reaches to the borders of heaven. 2 And to the north of the garden there is a sea of water, clear and pure to the taste, unlike anything else; so that, through the clearness one may look into the depths of the earth. 3 And when a man washes himself in it, he becomes perfectly clean and perfectly white, even if he were dark. 4 And God created that sea of his own good pleasure, for He knew what would come of the man He would make; so that after he had left the garden, because of his transgression, men should be born in the earth. Among them are righteous ones who will die, whose souls God would raise at the last day when all of them will return to their flesh, bathe in the water of that sea, and repent of their sins. 5 But when God caused Adam go out of the garden, He did not place him on the border of it northward. This was so that he and Eve would not be able to go near to the sea of water where they could wash themselves in it and be cleansed from their sins and erase the transgression they had committed, so that they be no longer reminded of it in the thought of their punishment. 6 As to the

southern side of the garden, God did not want Adam to live there either, because, when the wind blew from the north, it would bring to him, on that southern side, the delicious smell of the trees of the garden. 7 So God did not put Adam there. This was so that he would not be able to smell the sweet smell of those trees and forget his transgression, and find consolation for what he had done by taking delight in the smell of the trees and yet not be cleansed from his transgression. 8 Also, because God is merciful and of great pity, and governs all things in a way that He alone knows He made our father Adam to live in the western border of the garden because on that side the land is very wide. 9 And God commanded him to live there in a cave in a rock. This was the Cave of Treasures, which is below the garden.

Chapter II

1 But when our father Adam, and Eve, went out of the garden, they walked the ground on their feet, not knowing where they were going. 2 And when they came to the opening of the gate of the garden and saw the land spread before them widely, covered with stones large and small, and with sand, they feared and trembled, and fell on their faces from the fear that came over them and they were as though they were dead. 3 Until this time they had been in the garden land, beautifully planted with all manner of trees and they now saw themselves in a strange land, which they did not know and had never seen. 4 When they were in the garden they were filled with the

grace of a bright nature, and they had hearts not turned toward earthly things. 5 Therefore God had pity on them; and when He saw them fallen before the gate of the garden, He sent His Word to our father Adam, and to Eve, and raised them from their fallen state.

Chapter III

1 God said to Adam, "I have ordained days and years on this earth, and you and your descendants shall live and walk in them until the days and years are fulfilled. Then I shall send the Word that created you and against which you have transgressed the Word that made you come out of the garden and that raised you when you were fallen. 2 Yes, this is the Word that will again save you when the five and a half days are fulfilled." 3 But when Adam heard these words from God, and of the great five and a half days he did not understand the meaning of them. 4 For Adam was thinking there would be only five and a half days for him until the end of the world. 5 And Adam cried and prayed to God to explain it to him. 6 Then God in his mercy for Adam who was made after His own image and likeness explained to him that these were 5,000 and 500 years and how (the) One would then come and save him and his descendants. 7 But before that, God had made this covenant with our father, Adam, in the same terms before he came out of the garden, when he was by the tree where Eve took of the fruit and gave it to him to eat. 8 Because, when our father, Adam, came out of the garden he passed by that tree and saw how God had changed the appearance of it into

another form and how it had shriveled. 9 And as Adam went to it he feared, trembled, and fell down. But God in His mercy lifted him up and then made this covenant with him. 10 Also, when Adam was by the gate of the garden he saw the cherub with a sword of flashing fire in his hand, and the cherub grew angry and frowned at him. Both Adam and Eve became afraid of the cherub and thought he meant to put them to death. So they fell on their faces, trembling with fear. 11 But he had pity on them and showed them mercy. And turning from them, he went up to heaven and prayed to the Lord, and said; 12 "Lord, You sent me to watch at the gate of the garden, with a sword of fire. 13 But when Your servants, Adam and Eve, saw me, they fell on their faces, and were as dead. O my Lord, what shall we do to Your servants?" 14 Then God had pity on them, and showed them mercy, and sent His Angel to keep the garden. 15 And the Word of the Lord came to Adam and Eve, and raised them up. 16 And the Lord said to Adam, "I told you that at the end of the five and a half days I will send my Word and save you. 17 Therefore, strengthen your heart and stay in the Cave of Treasures, of which I have spoken to you before." 18 And when Adam heard this Word from God he was comforted with that which God had told him. For He had told him how He would save him.

Author's note: The year 1740 equates to the Hebrew year 5500. It was around this time the Great Revival or the Great Awakening began in the United States and lasted until around 1750. Some sources have the religious revival at 1678 – 1745 while other sources have 1740 – 1750. However, the time between creation and Adam's fall must be accounted for. The author is suggesting that the time between the fall of Adam and the death of Christ is 5500 years.

Chapter IV

1 But Adam and Eve cried for having come out of the garden, which was their first home. 2 And indeed, when Adam looked at his flesh he saw that it was altered, and he cried bitterly, he and Eve cried, over what they had done. And they walked and went gently down into the Cave of Treasures. 3 And as they came to it, Adam cried over himself and said to Eve, "Look at this cave that is to be our prison in this world, and a place of punishment! 4 What is it compared with the garden? What is its narrowness compared with the space of the other? 5 What is this rock compared of those groves? What is the gloom of this cavern, compared with the light of the garden? 6 What is this overhanging ledge of rock that shelters us compared with the mercy of the Lord that overshadowed us? 7 What is the soil of this cave compared with the garden land? Does this earth, scattered with stones, compared to that garden planted with delicious fruit trees?" 8 And Adam said to Eve, "Look at your eyes, and at mine, which before beheld angels praising in heaven without ceasing. 9 Now we do not see as we did; our eyes have become of flesh; they cannot see like they saw before." 10 Adam said again to Eve, "What is our body today, compared to what it was in former days, when we lived in the garden?" 11 After this, Adam did not want to enter the cave under

the overhanging rock. He never wanted to enter it again. 12 But he bowed to God's commands; and said to himself, "Unless I enter the cave, I shall again be a transgressor."

Chapter V

1 Then Adam and Eve entered the cave, and stood praying, in their own tongue, unknown to us, but which they knew well. 2 And as they prayed, Adam raised his eyes and saw the rock and the roof of the cave that covered him overhead. This prevented him from seeing either heaven or God's creatures. So he cried and beat his chest hard, until he dropped, and was as dead. 3 And Eve sat crying; for she believed he was dead. 4 Then she got up, spread her hands toward God, appealing to Him for mercy and pity, and said, "O God, forgive me my sin, the sin which I committed, and don't remember it against me. 5 For I alone caused Your servant to fall from the garden into this condemned land; from light into this darkness; and from the house of joy into this prison. 6 O God, look at this Your servant fallen in this manner, and bring him back to life, that he may cry and repent of his transgression which he committed through (because of) me. 7 Don't take away his soul at this time; but let him live so that he may stand after the measure of his repentance, and do Your will, as before his death. 8 But if You do not bring him back to life, then, O God, take away my own soul, so that I will be like him, and leave me not in this dungeon, alone; for I could not stand alone in this world, without him. 9 For You, O God, caused him to fall asleep, and took a bone

from his side, and placed the flesh back in its place by Your divine power. 10 And You took me, the bone, and made me, a woman, bright like him, with heart, reason, and speech; and flesh like to his own; and You made me after the likeness of his looks, by Your mercy and power. 11 O Lord, I and he are one, and You, O God, are our Creator, You are He who made us both in one day. 12 Therefore, O God, give him life so that he may be with me in this strange land while we live in it due to our transgression. 13 But if You will not give him life, then take me, even me, like him; that we both may die the same day." 14 And Eve cried bitterly, and fell on our father, Adam, because of her great sorrow.

Chapter VI

1 But God looked at them, for they had killed themselves through great grief. 2 And He decided to raise them and comfort them. 3 Therefore, He sent His Word to them that they should stand and be raised immediately. 4 And the Lord said to Adam and Eve, "You transgressed of your own free will, until you came out of the garden in which I had placed you. 5 Of your own free will have you transgressed through your desire for divinity, greatness, and an exalted state, such as I have; therefore I deprived you of the bright nature which you had then, and I made you come out of the garden to this land, rough and full of trouble. 6 If only you had not transgressed My commandment and had kept My law, and had not eaten of the fruit of the tree which I told you not to come near! And

there were fruit trees in the garden better than that one. 7 But the wicked Satan did not keep his faith and had no good intent towards Me, and although I had created him he considered Me to be useless, and he sought the Godhead for himself. For this I hurled him down from heaven so that he could not remain in his first estate. It was he who made the tree appear pleasant to your eyes until you ate of it by believing his words. 8 Thus have you transgressed My commandment, and therefore I have brought on you all these sorrows. 9 For I am God the Creator, who, when I created My creatures, did not intend to destroy them. But after they had greatly roused My anger I punished them with grievous plagues until they repent. 10 But, if on the contrary they still continue hardened in their transgression they shall be under a curse forever."

Chapter VII

1 When Adam and Eve heard these words from God, they cried and sobbed even more, but they strengthened their hearts in God because they now felt that the Lord was to them like a father and a mother; and for this very reason, they cried before Him, and sought mercy from Him. 2 Then God had pity on them, and said: "O Adam, I have made My covenant with you, and I will not turn from it; neither will I let you return to the garden, until My covenant of the great five and a half days is fulfilled." 3 Then Adam said to God, "O Lord, You created us, and made us fit to be in the garden; and before I transgressed, You made all beasts come to me, that I should name

them. 4 Your grace was then on me; and I named every one according to Your mind; and you made them all subject to me. 5 But now, O Lord God, that I have transgressed Your commandment, all beasts will rise against me and will devour me, and Eve Your handmaid; and will cut off our life from the face of the earth. 6 I therefore beg you, O God, that since You have made us come out of the garden, and have made us be in a strange land, You will not let the beasts hurt us." 7 When the Lord heard these words from Adam, He had pity on him, and felt that he had truly said that the beasts of the field would rise and devour him and Eve, because He, the Lord, was angry with the two of them because of their transgressions. 8 Then God commanded the beasts, and the birds, and all that moves on the earth, to come to Adam and to be familiar with him, and not to trouble him and Eve; nor any of the good and righteous among their offspring. 9 Then all the beasts paid homage to Adam, according to the commandment of God except the serpent, against which God was angry. It did not come to Adam, with the beasts.

Chapter VIII

1 Then Adam cried and said, "O God, when we lived in the garden, and our hearts were lifted up, we saw the angels that sang praises in heaven, but now we can't see like we once saw. No. When we entered the cave all creation became hidden from us." 2 Then God the Lord said to Adam, "When you were under subjection to Me, you had a bright nature within you and for that reason could you see

distant things. But after you transgressed your bright nature was taken out of you and it was not left in you to see distant things, but only things near to you, as is the ability of the flesh, for it is brutish." 3 When Adam and Eve had heard these words from God, they went their way, praising and worshipping Him with a sorrowful heart. 4 And God ceased communing with them.

Chapter IX

1 Then Adam and Eve came out of the Cave of Treasures, and came near to the garden gate. There they stood and looked at it and cried for having gone away from it. 2 And Adam and Eve went south of the gate of the garden to the side of it and found there the water that watered the garden, which came from the root of the Tree of Life, and they saw that the water was split from there into four rivers over the earth. 3 Then they came near to that water and looked at it and saw that it was the water that came up from under the root of the Tree of Life in the garden. 4 And Adam cried and wailed, and beat his chest for being cut out from the garden; and said to Eve: 5 "Why have you brought so many of these plagues and punishments on me, on yourself, and on our descendants?" 6 And Eve said to him, "What is it you have seen that has caused you to cry and to speak to me in this manner?" 7 And he said to Eve, "Do you not see this water that watered the trees of the garden, and flowed out from there that was with us in the garden? 8 And when we were in the garden we did not care about it, but since we came to this strange land we love it and

turn it to use for our body." 9 But when Eve heard these words from him, she cried; and from the soreness of their crying, they fell into that water; and would have put an end to themselves in it so as never again to return and behold the creation for when they looked at the work of creation, they felt they must put an end to themselves.

Chapter X

1 Then God, merciful and gracious, looked at them as they were lying in the water, and close to death, and He sent an angel who brought them out of the water and laid them on the seashore as dead. 2 Then the angel went up to God and said, "O God, Your creatures have breathed their last breath." 3 Then God sent His Word to Adam and Eve, who raised them from their death. 4 And Adam said, after he was raised, "O God, while we were in the garden we did not require or care about this water, but since we came to this land we cannot do without it." 5 Then God said to Adam, "While you were under My command and were a bright angel you did not experience this water. 6 But now that you have transgressed My commandment, you can not do without water to wash your body and make it grow, for it is now like that of beasts, and is in want of water." 7 When Adam and Eve heard these words from God, they cried a bitter cry; and Adam entreated God to let him return into the garden and look at it a second time. 8 But God said to Adam, "I have made you a promise; when that promise is fulfilled, I will bring you back into the garden, you and your righteous descendants." 9 And God ceased to

commune with Adam.

Authors note: Notice the text promises Adam and his righteous descendants will be returned to Eden after the 5,500 year term is completed. Thus, the righteous portion of mankind would be returned in the Hebrew year 5,500 plus the time between creation and Adam's fall. Adam must be kept alive or transfigured since resurrection of the body was not part of Jewish doctrine.

Chapter XI

1 Adam and Eve then felt themselves burning with thirst, and heat, and sorrow. 2 And Adam said to Eve, "We shall not drink of this water even if we were to die. O Eve, when this water comes into our inner parts it will increase our punishments and that of our descendants." 3 Both Adam and Eve then went away from the water, and drank none of it at all but came and entered the Cave of Treasures. 4 But when in it Adam could not see Eve he only heard the noise she made. Neither could she see Adam, but heard the noise he made. 5 Then Adam cried in deep affliction and beat his chest, and he got up and said to Eve, "Where are you?" 6 And she said to him, "Look, I am standing here in this darkness." 7 He then said to her, "Remember the bright nature in which we lived, when we lived in the garden! 8 O Eve! Remember the glory that rested on us in the garden. O Eve! Remember the trees that overshadowed us in the garden while we moved among them. 9 O Eve! Remember that while we were in the garden, we knew neither night nor day. Think of the

Tree of Life. From below it flowed the water and that shed splendor over us! Remember, O Eve, the land of the garden and the brightness of it. 10 Think, oh think of that garden in which there was no darkness while we lived in it. 11 But no sooner did we come into this Cave of Treasures than darkness surrounded us all around until we can no longer see each other, and all the pleasure of this life has come to an end."

Chapter XII

1 Then Adam beat his chest, he and Eve, and they mourned the whole night until the first light of dawn, and they sighed over the length of the night in Miyazia. 2 And Adam beat himself, and threw himself on the ground in the cave, from bitter grief, and because of the darkness and lay there as dead. 3 But Eve heard the noise he made in falling on the ground. And she felt about for him with her hands and found him like a corpse. 4 Then she was afraid, speechless, and she remained by him. 5 But the merciful Lord looked on the death of Adam, and on Eve's silence from fear of the darkness. 6 And the Word of God came to Adam and raised him from his death, and opened Eve's mouth that she might speak. 7 Then Adam stood up in the cave and said, "O God, why has light departed from us and darkness covered us? Why did you leave us in this extensive darkness? Why do you plague us like this? 8 And this darkness, O Lord, where was it before it covered us? It is because of this that we cannot see each other. 9 For so long as we were in the garden we

neither saw nor even knew what darkness was. I was not hidden from Eve, neither was she hidden from me, until now that she cannot see me and no darkness came over us to separate us from each other. 10 But she and I were both in one bright light. I saw her and she saw me. Yet now since we came into this cave darkness has covered us and separated us from each other so that I do not see her, and she does not see me. 11 O Lord, will You then plague us with this darkness?"

Author's note: Miyazia equates to a particular month in the Ethiopian calendar.

Chapter XIII

1 Then when God, who is merciful and full of pity, heard Adam's voice, He said to him: 2 "O Adam, so long as the good angel was obedient to Me, a bright light rested on him and on his hosts. 3 But when he transgressed My commandment, I dispossessed him of that bright nature, and he became dark. 4 And when he was in the heavens, in the realms of light, he knew nothing of darkness. 5 But he transgressed, and I made him fall from the heaven onto the earth; and it was this darkness that came over him. 6 And, O Adam, while in My garden and obedient to Me that bright light rest also on you. 7 But when I heard of your transgression, I took from you that bright light. Yet, of My mercy, I did not turn you into darkness but I made your body a body of flesh over which I spread this skin in order that

it may bear cold and heat. 8 If I had let My wrath fall heavily on you I should have destroyed you and had I turned you into darkness it would have been as if I had killed you. 9 But in My mercy I have made you as you are when you transgressed My commandment, O Adam, I drove you from the garden, and made you come forth into this land and commanded you to live in this cave and darkness covered you, as it did over him who transgressed My commandment. 10 Thus, O Adam, has this night deceived you. It is not to last forever but is only of twelve hours when it is over daylight will return. 11 Do not sigh or be moved and do not say in your heart that this darkness is long and drags on wearily. Do not say in your heart that I plague you with it. 12 Strengthen your heart and be not afraid. This darkness is not a punishment. Adam, I have made the day and have placed the sun in it to give light in order that you and your children should do your work. 13 For I knew you would sin and transgress and come out into this land. Yet I wouldn't force you nor ride heard over you, nor shut up, nor doom you through your fall, nor through your coming out from light into darkness, nor yet through your coming from the garden into this land. 14 For I made you of the light and I willed to bring out children of light from you that were like you. 15 But you did not keep My commandment one day until I had finished the creation and blessed everything in it. 16 Then, concerning the tree, I commanded you not to eat of it. Yet I knew that Satan, who deceived himself, would also deceive you. 17 So I made known to you by means of the tree, not to come near him. And I told you not to eat of the fruit thereof, nor to taste of it, nor yet to sit under it, nor to yield to it. 18 Had I not spoken to you, O Adam, concerning the tree and had I left you without a commandment and you had sinned it would have been an offence on My part, for not having given you any order you would turn around and blame Me for it. 19 But I commanded you, and warned you, and you fell. So that My creatures cannot blame Me; but the blame rests on them alone. 20 And, O Adam, I have made the day so that you and your descendants can work and toil in it. And I have made the night for them to rest in it from their work and for the beasts of the field to go forth by night and look for their food. 21 But little of darkness now remains, O Adam, and daylight will soon appear."

Chapter XIV

1 Then Adam said to God: "O Lord, take my soul and let me not see this gloom any more, or remove me to some place where there is no darkness." 2 But God the Lord said to Adam, " I say to you, indeed, this darkness will pass from you every day, I have determined for you until the fulfillment of My covenant when I will save you and bring you back again into the garden and into the house of light you long for, in which there is no darkness. I will bring you to it in the kingdom of heaven." 3 Again God said to Adam, "All this misery that you have been made to take on yourself because of your transgression will not free you from the hand of Satan and it will not save you. 4 But I will. When I shall come down from heaven and shall become flesh of your descendants, and take on Myself the

23

infirmity from which you suffer then the darkness that covered you in this cave shall cover Me in the grave, when I am in the flesh of your descendants. 5 And I, who am without years, shall be subject to the reckoning of years of times of months, and of days, and I shall be reckoned as one of the sons of men in order to save you." 6 And God ceased to commune with Adam.

Author's Note: John 1:14And the Word was made flesh, and dwelt among us, (and we beheld his glory, the glory as of the only begotten of the Father,) full of grace and truth.
John 12:46 American King James Version: I am come a light into the world, that whoever believes on me should not abide in darkness.

Chapter XV

1 Then Adam and Eve cried and was sorrowful because of God's word to them, that they should not return to the garden until the fulfillment of the days decreed on them, but mostly because God had told them that He should suffer for their salvation.

Chapter XVI

1 After this, Adam and Eve continued to stand in the cave, praying and crying, until the morning dawned on them. 2 And when they saw the light returned to them they refrained from being afraid and strengthened their hearts. 3 Then Adam came out of the cave. And

when he came to the mouth of it and stood and turned his face towards the east and saw the sunrise in glowing rays and felt the heat thereof on his body, he was afraid of it and thought in his heart that this flame came forth to plague him. 4 He then cried and beat his chest and he fell on the ground on his face and made his appeal saying: 5 "O Lord, plague me not, neither consume me, nor yet take away my life from the earth." 6 For he thought the sun was God. 7 Because while he was in the garden and heard the voice of God and the sound He made in the garden, and feared Him, Adam never saw the brilliant light of the sun, neither did its flaming heat touch his body. 8 Therefore he was afraid of the sun when flaming rays of it reached him. He thought God meant to plague him with it all the days He had decreed for him. 9 For Adam also said in his thoughts, that God did not plague them with darkness but He had caused this sun to rise and to plague them with burning heat. 10 But while he was thinking like this in his heart the Word of God came to him and said: 11 " Adam, get up on your feet. This sun is not God, but it has been created to give light by day that I spoke to you about in the cave saying, 'The dawn would come, and there would be light by day.' 12 But I am God who comforted you in the night." 13 And God ceased to commune with Adam.

Chapter XVII

1 Then, Adam and Eve came out at the mouth of the cave and went toward the garden. 2 But as they went near the western gate, from

which Satan came when he deceived Adam and Eve, they found the
serpent that became Satan coming at the gate, and it was sorrowfully
licking the dust, and wiggling on its breast on the ground because of
the curse that fell on it from God. 3 Before the curse the serpent was
the most exalted of all beasts, now it was changed and become
slippery and the meanest of them all, and it crept on its breast and
went on its belly. 4 Before, it was the fairest of all beasts. It had been
changed and became the most ugly of them all. Instead of feeding on
the best food, now it turned to eat the dust. Instead of living as
before, in the best places, now it lived in the dust. 5 It had been the
most beautiful of all beasts, and all stood speechless at its beauty, it
was now abhorred of them. 6 And, again, whereas it lived in a
beautiful home, to which all other animals came from everywhere;
and where it drank, they drank also of the same; now, after it had
become venomous, by reason of God's curse, all beasts fled from its
home and would not drink of the water it drank, but fled from it.

Chapter XVIII

1 When the accursed serpent saw Adam and Eve it swelled its head,
stood on its tail, and with eyes blood- red, it acted like it would kill
them. 2 It made straight for Eve and ran after her while Adam stood
by and yelled because he had no stick in his hand with which to hit
the serpent, and did not know how to put it to death. 3 But with a
heart burning for Eve, Adam approached the serpent and held it by
the tail. When it turned towards him and said to him: 4 "O Adam,

because of you and Eve I am slippery, and go on my belly." Then with its great strength it threw down Adam and Eve and squeezed them, and tried to kill them. 5 But God sent an angel who threw the serpent away from them, and raised them up. 6 Then the Word of God came to the serpent, and said to it, "The first time I made you slick, and made you to go on your belly but I did not deprive you of speech. 7 This time, however, you will be mute, and you and your race will speak no more because, the first time My creatures were ruined because of you, and this time you tried to kill them." 8 Then the serpent was struck mute, and it was no longer able to speak. 9 And a wind blew down from heaven by the command of God and carried away the serpent from Adam and Eve and threw it on the seashore where it landed in India.

Chapter XIX

1 But Adam and Eve cried before God. And Adam said to Him: 2 "O Lord, when I was in the cave I said this to you, my Lord, the beasts of the field would rise and devour me and cut off my life from the earth." 3 Then Adam, because of what had happened to him, beat his chest and fell on the ground like a corpse. Then the Word of God came to him, who raised him, and said to him, 4 "O Adam, not one of these beasts will be able to hurt you because I have made the beasts and other moving things come to you in the cave. I did not let the serpent come with them because it might have risen against you and made you tremble and the fear of it should fall into your hearts. 5 I

knew that the accursed one is wicked; therefore I would not let it come near you with the other beasts. 6 But now strengthen your heart and fear not. I am with you to the end of the days I have determined for you."

Chapter XX

1 Then Adam cried and said, "O God, take us away to some other place, where the serpent can not come near us again and rise against us. For I fear that it might find your handmaid Eve alone and kill her, for its eyes are hideous and evil." 2 But God said to Adam and Eve, " Don't be afraid. From now on, I will not let it come near you. I have driven it away from you and from this mountain. I will not leave in it the ability to hurt you." 3 Then Adam and Eve worshipped before God and gave Him thanks and praised Him for having delivered them from death.

Chapter XXI

1 Then Adam and Eve went in search of the garden. 2 And the heat beat like a flame on their faces and they sweated from the heat. And they cried before the Lord. 3 But the place where they cried was close to a high mountain (top) that faced the western gate of the garden. 4 Then Adam threw himself down from the top of that mountain. His face was torn and his flesh was ripped and he lost much of his blood and was close to death. 5 Meanwhile Eve remained standing on the

mountain crying over him lying as he was. 6 And she said, "I don't wish to live after him, for all that he did to himself was because of me." 7 Then she threw herself after him; and was torn and ripped by stones and remained lying as dead. 8 But the merciful God, who looks over His creatures, looked at Adam and Eve as they lay dead, and He sent His Word to them and raised them. 9 And said to Adam, "O Adam, all this misery, which you have brought on yourself, will have no affect on My ruling, neither will it alter the covenant of the five thousand and five hundred (5,500) years."

Chapter XXII

1 Then Adam said to God, "I dry up in the heat, I am faint from walking, and I don't want to be in this world. And I don't know when You will let me rest and take me out of it." 2 Then the Lord God said to him, "O Adam, it cannot be now, not until you have ended your days. Then I shall bring you out of this miserable land." 3 And Adam said to God, "While I was in the garden I knew neither heat, nor fatigue, neither transience, nor trembling, nor fear; but now since I came to this land, all this affliction has come over me. 4 Then God said to Adam, "So long as you were keeping My commandment, My light and My grace rested on you. But when you transgressed My commandment, sorrow and misery came to you in this land." 5 And Adam cried and said, "O Lord, do not cut me off for this, neither punish me with heavy plagues, nor yet repay me according to my sin; for we, of our own will, transgressed Your commandment and

29

ignored Your law and tried to become gods like you when Satan the enemy deceived us." 6 Then God said again to Adam, "Because you have endured fear and trembling in this land of fatigue and suffering, treading and walking about, going on this mountain, and dying from it, I will take all this on Myself in order to save you."

Author's note:

Isaiah 53

1 Who hath believed our report? and to whom is the arm of the LORD revealed?

2 For he shall grow up before him as a tender plant, and as a root out of a dry ground: he hath no form nor comeliness; and when we shall see him, there is no beauty that we should desire him.

3 He is despised and rejected of men; a man of sorrows, and acquainted with grief: and we hid as it were our faces from him; he was despised, and we esteemed him not.

4 Surely he hath borne our griefs, and carried our sorrows: yet we did esteem him stricken, smitten of God, and afflicted.

5 But he was wounded for our transgressions, he was bruised for our iniquities: the chastisement of our peace was upon him; and with his stripes we are healed.

6 All we like sheep have gone astray; we have turned every one to his own way; and the LORD hath laid on him the iniquity of us all.

7 He was oppressed, and he was afflicted, yet he opened not his mouth: he is brought as a lamb to the slaughter, and as a sheep before her shearers is dumb, so he openeth not his mouth.

8 He was taken from prison and from judgment: and who shall declare his generation? for he was cut off out of the land of the living: for the transgression of my people was he stricken.

9 And he made his grave with the wicked, and with the rich in his death; because he had done no violence, neither was any deceit in his mouth.

10 Yet it pleased the LORD to bruise him; he hath put him to grief: when thou shalt make his soul an offering for sin, he shall see his seed, he shall prolong his days, and the pleasure of the LORD shall prosper in his hand.

11 He shall see of the travail of his soul, and shall be satisfied: by his knowledge shall my righteous servant justify many; for he shall bear their iniquities.

Chapter XXIII

1 Then Adam cried more and said, "O God, have mercy on me and do not take on yourself that which I will do." 2 But God withdrew His Word from Adam and Eve. 3 Then Adam and Eve stood on their feet and Adam said to Eve, "Strengthen yourself, and I also will strengthen myself." And she strengthened herself as Adam told her. 4 Then Adam and Eve took stones and placed them in the shape of an altar and they took leaves from the trees outside the garden, with which they wiped from the face of the rock the blood they had spilled. 5 But that which had dropped on the sand they took together with the dust with which it was mixed and offered it on the altar as an offering to God. 6 Then Adam and Eve stood under the Altar and cried, praying to God, "Forgive us our offense and our sin, and look

at us with Your eye of mercy. For when we were in the garden our praises and our hymns went up before you without ceasing. 7 But when we came into this strange land, pure praise was no longer ours, nor righteous prayer, nor understanding hearts, nor sweet thoughts, nor wise judgment, nor long discernment, nor upright feelings, neither was our bright nature left within us. But our body is changed from the likeness in which it was at first when we were created. 8 Yet now look at our blood which is offered on these stones and accept it at our hands as if it were the praise we used to sing to you at first when we were in the garden." 9 And Adam began to make more requests of God. Our Father, Who are in Heaven, be gracious unto us. O Lord, our God, hallowed be Your Name and let the remembrance of You be glorified in Heaven above and upon earth here below. Let Your kingdom reign over us now and forever. The Holy Men of old said remit and forgive unto all men whatsoever they have done unto me. And lead us not into temptation, but deliver us from the evil thing; for Your is the kingdom and You shall reign in glory forever and forevermore, AMEN.

Author's note: Verse 4 and continuing to the end of the chapter contain and present ideas that are of an obviously Christian era. There would have been no "men of old" at the time of Adam and Eve. The text parallels the Lord's Prayer. This, and other references to Christian symbols, makes the dating of the text at about the 3rd century A.D. likely.

Matthew 6: 9

9 After this manner therefore pray ye: Our Father which art in heaven, Hallowed be your name.

10 Thy kingdom come, Thy will be done in earth, as it is in heaven.

11 Give us this day our daily bread.

12 And forgive us our debts, as we forgive our debtors.

13 And lead us not into temptation, but deliver us from evil: For thine is the kingdom, and the power, and the glory, for ever. Amen. 14 For if ye forgive men their trespasses, your heavenly Father will also forgive you: 15 But if ye forgive not men their trespasses, neither will your Father forgive your trespasses.

Chapter XXIV

1 Then the merciful God, who is good and a lover of men, looked at Adam and Eve and at their blood, which they had held up as an offering to Him without an order from Him for so doing. But He wondered at them and accepted their offering. 2 And God sent from His presence a bright fire that consumed their offering. 3 He smelled the sweet savor of their offering and showed them mercy. 4 Then the Word of God came to Adam, and said to him, "O Adam, as you have shed your blood so will I shed My own blood when I become flesh of your descendants. And as you died, O Adam, so also will I die. And as you built an altar, so also will I make for you an altar of the earth. And as you offered your blood on it, so also will I offer My blood on

an altar on the earth. 5 And as you appealed for forgiveness through that blood, so also will I make My blood forgiveness of sins and erase transgressions in it. 6 And now, behold, I have accepted your offering, O Adam, but the days of the covenant in which I have bound you are not fulfilled. When they are fulfilled, then will I bring you back into the garden. 7 Now, therefore, strengthen your heart. And when sorrow comes over you make Me an offering and I will be favorable to you."

Chapter XXV

1 But God knew that Adam believed he would frequently kill himself and make an offering to Him of his blood. 2 Therefore He said to him, "Adam, don't ever kill yourself like this again, by throwing yourself down from that mountain." 3 But Adam said to God, "I was thinking to put an end to myself right now for having transgressed Your commandments and for my having come out of the beautiful garden and for the bright light which You have taken from me, and for the praises which poured out from my mouth without ceasing, and for the light that covered me. 4 Yet because of Your goodness, O God, you did not get rid of me altogether, but you have been favorable to me every time I die and you bring me to life. 5 And thereby it will be made known that You are a merciful God who does not want anyone to perish, who would love it if no one should fall, and who does not condemn any one cruelly, badly, or by total destruction." 6 Then Adam remained silent. 7 And the Word of God

came to him and blessed him and comforted him and covenanted with him that He would save him at the end of the days determined for him. 8 This, then, was the first offering Adam made to God and so it became his custom to do.

Chapter XXVI

1 Then Adam took Eve and they began to return to the Cave of Treasures where they lived. But when they got closer to it and saw it from a distance, heavy sorrow fell on Adam and Eve when they looked at it. 2 Then Adam said to Eve, "When we were on the mountain we were comforted by the Word of God that talked with us and the light that came from the east shown over us. 3 But now the Word of God is hidden from us and the light that shined over us has changed so much that it has disappeared and let darkness and sorrow cover us. 4 And we are forced to enter this cave that is like a prison, in which darkness covers us so that we are separated from each other. You cannot see me. I cannot see you." 5 When Adam had said these words, they cried and spread their hands before God because they were full of sorrow. 6 And they prayed to God to bring the sun for them to shine on them so that darkness would not return to them and that they wouldn't have to go under this covering of rock. They wanted to die rather than see the darkness. 7 Then God looked at Adam and Eve and at their great sorrow and all they had done with a fervent heart because of all the trouble they were in. When compared to their former state of well-being, all the misery

that came over them did so in this strange land. 8 Therefore God was neither angry with them nor impatient, but he was patient and longsuffering toward them, as toward the children He had created. 9 Then the Word of God came to Adam and said to him, "Adam, regarding the sun, if I were to take it and bring it to you, days, hours, years and months would all stop and the covenant I have made with you, would never be fulfilled. 10 And you would be deserted and stuck in a perpetual plague and you would never be saved. 11 Yes, rather, bear up long, and calm your soul while you live night and day until the fulfillment of the days and the time of My covenant has come. 12 Then I shall come and save you, Adam. I do not wish for you to be afflicted. 13 And when I look at all the good things that you lived in before, and why you came out of them, then I am willing to show you mercy. 14 But I cannot alter the covenant that has gone out of My mouth, otherwise I would have brought you back into the garden. 15 However, when the covenant is fulfilled then I will show you and your descendants mercy, and bring you into a land of gladness where there is neither sorrow nor suffering but abiding joy and gladness, and light that never fails, and praises that never cease, and a beautiful garden that shall never pass away." 16 And God said again to Adam, "Be patient and enter the cave because of the darkness of which you were afraid shall only be twelve hours long. When it is over, light will come up." 17 Then when Adam heard these words from God, he and Eve worshipped before Him, and their hearts were comforted. They returned into the cave after their custom, while tears flowed from their eyes sorrow and wailing came from their hearts and they wished their soul would leave their body. 18 And Adam and Eve stood praying until the darkness of night covered them and Adam was hidden from Eve and she from him. 19 And they remained standing in prayer.

Chapter XXVII

1 Satan, the hater of all that is good, saw how they continued in prayer, and how God communed with them, and comforted them, and how He had accepted their offering. Then Satan made a phantasm. 2 He began by transforming his hosts. In his hands was a shining, glimmering fire, and they were in a huge light. 3 Then, he placed his throne near the mouth of the cave, because he could not enter it due to their prayers. And he shown light into the cave until the cave glistened over Adam and Eve while his hosts began to sing praises. 4 Satan did this so that when Adam saw the light he would think to himself that it was a heavenly light and that Satan's hosts were angels and that God had sent them to watch at the cave, and give him light in the darkness. 5 Satan planned that when Adam came out of the cave and saw them and Adam and Eve bowed to Satan, then he would overcome Adam and humble him before God a second time. 6 When, therefore, Adam and Eve saw the light, thinking it was real, they strengthened their hearts. Then, as they were trembling, Adam said to Eve: 7 "Look at that great light, and at those many songs of praise, and at that host standing outside who won't come into our cave. Why don't they tell us what they want or

where they are from or what the meaning of this light is or what those praises are or why they have been sent to this place, and why they won't come in? 8 If they were from God, they would come into the cave with us and would tell us why they were sent." 9 Then Adam stood up and prayed to God with a burning heart and said: 10 "O Lord, is there in the world another god besides You who created angels and filled them with light, and sent them to keep us, who would come with them? 11 But, look, we see these hosts that stand at the mouth of the cave. They are in a great light and they sing loud praises. If they are of some other god(s) than You, tell me, and if they are sent by you, inform me of the reason for which You have sent them." 12 No sooner had Adam said this, than an angel from God appeared to him in the cave, who said to him, "O Adam, fear not. This is Satan and his hosts. He wishes to deceive you as he deceived you at first. For the first time, he was hidden in the serpent, but this time he is come to you in the likeness of an angel of light in order that, when you worshipped him, he might enslave you in the very presence of God." 13 Then the angel went from Adam and seized Satan at the opening of the cave, and stripped him of the false image (lie / pretense) he had assumed and brought him in his own hideous form to Adam and Eve who were afraid of him when they saw him. 14 And the angel said to Adam, "This hideous form has been his ever since God made him fall from heaven. He could not have come near you in it. Therefore, he transformed himself into an angel of light." 15 Then the angel drove Satan and his hosts away from Adam and Eve and said to them, "Fear not. God who created you will strengthen you." 16 And the angel left them. 17 But Adam and Eve remained standing in the cave and no consolation came to them as they were divided in their thoughts. 18 And when it was morning they prayed and then went out to seek the garden, for their hearts were seeking it, and they could get no consolation for having left it.

Chapter XXVIII

1 But when the crafty Satan saw that they were going to the garden he gathered together his host and came in appearance on a cloud, intent on deceiving them. 2 But when Adam and Eve saw him in a vision, they thought they were angels of God come to comfort them about having left the garden, or to bring them back again into it. 3 And Adam spread his hands before God, begged Him to make him understand what they were. 4 Then Satan, the hater of all that is good, said to Adam, "O Adam, I am an angel of the great God and, behold the hosts that surround me. 5 God has sent us to take you and bring you to the northern border of the garden to the shore of the clear sea, and bathe you and Eve in it, and raise you to your former joy, that you return to the garden once again." 6 These words sank into the heart of Adam and Eve. 7 Yet God withheld His Word from Adam, and did not make him understand at once but waited to see his strength and whether he would be overcome as Eve was when in the garden, or whether he would win this battle. 8 Then Satan called to Adam and Eve and said, "Behold, we go to the sea of water," and they began to go. 9 And Adam and Eve followed them at little

distance. 10 But when they came to the mountain to the north of the garden which was a very high mountain without any steps to the top of it, the Devil came near to Adam and Eve, and made them go up to the top in reality and not in a vision, because he wished to throw them down and kill them, and to wipe their names from the earth, so that this earth should belong to him and his hosts alone.

Chapter XXIX

1 But when the merciful God saw that Satan wished to kill Adam with his many tricks, and saw that Adam was meek and without guile, God spoke to Satan in a loud voice, and cursed him. 2 Then he and his hosts fled, and Adam and Eve remained standing on the top of the mountain, from there they saw below them the wide world, high above which they were. But they saw none of the host which time after time were by them. 3 They cried, both Adam and Eve, before God, and begged for forgiveness of Him. 4 Then the Word from God came to Adam, and said to him, "You must know and understand concerning this Satan, that he seeks to deceive you and your descendants after you." 5 And Adam cried before the Lord God, and begged and prayed to Him to give him something from the garden, as a token to him, wherein to be comforted. 6 And God considered Adam's thought, and sent the angel Michael as far as the sea that reaches India, to take from there golden rods and bring them to Adam. 7 This God did in His wisdom in order that these golden rods, being with Adam in the cave, should shine forth with light in

the night around him, and put an end to his fear of the darkness. 8 Then the angel Michael went down by God's order, took golden rods, as God had commanded him, and brought them to God.

Author's note: God spoke to Adam concerning "this Satan," a turn of phrase that leads one to believe there are other Satans. Based on the meaning of the word satan, there is no limit to the number of satans one could have. Satan is derived from Hebrew, satan meaning "adversary". Satan, or the Devil, plays various evil roles in ancient and modern literature and in Jewish, Christian, Muslim and Zoroastrian religious traditions. Satan is an opponent of God and of those seeking to do God's will. He is often described as an angel named Lucifer who was cast out of heaven for rebelling against God, was condemned to roam the earth and rule hell, and who battles God for possession of souls and the earth. That legend is not found as such in the Bible but is based on interpretations of scattered Bible passages and later literary portrayals.

The English word "Satan" is from a Hebrew word meaning "to oppose" or "adversary." "Devil" is from the Greek diabolos , meaning "to slander or accuse." The name "Lucifer" appears in Isaiah 14 in the King James Version of the Bible

Chapter XXX

1 After these things, God commanded the angel Gabriel to go down to the garden and say to the cherub who kept it, "Behold, God has commanded me to come into the garden, and to take from it sweet

smelling incense and give it to Adam." 2 Then the angel Gabriel went down by God's order to the garden and told the cherub as God had commanded him. 3 The cherub then said, "This is acceptable." And Gabriel went in and took the incense. 4 Then God commanded his angel Raphael to go down to the garden, and speak to the cherub about some myrrh to give to Adam. 5 And the angel Raphael went down and told the cherub as God had commanded him, and the cherub said, "This is acceptable." Then Raphael went in and took the myrrh. 6 The golden rods were from the Indian sea, where there are precious stones. The incense was from the eastern border of the garden, and the myrrh from the western border, from where bitterness came over Adam. 7 And the angels brought these things to God, by the Tree of Life, in the garden. 8 Then God said to the angels, "Dip them in the spring of water, then take them and sprinkle their water over Adam and Eve, that they should be a little comforted in their sorrow, and give them to Adam and Eve. 9 And the angels did as God had commanded them, and they gave all those things to Adam and Eve on the top of the mountain on which Satan had placed them, when he sought to make an end of them. 10 And when Adam saw the golden rods, the incense and the myrrh, he rejoiced and cried because he thought that the gold was a token of the kingdom from where he had come and the incense was a token of the bright light which had been taken from him, and that the myrrh was a token of the sorrow which he was in.

Chapter XXXI

1 After these things happened, God said to Adam, "You asked Me for something from the garden to be comforted with, and I have given you these three tokens as a consolation to you so that you trust in Me and in My covenant with you. 2 For I will come and save you and when I am in the flesh, kings shall bring me gold, incense, and myrrh. Gold is a token of My kingdom, incense is a token of My divinity, and myrrh is a token of My suffering and of My death. 3 But, Adam, put these by you in the cave, the gold so that it may shine light over you by night, the incense so that you smell its sweet savor, and the myrrh to comfort you in your sorrow." 4 When Adam heard these words from God, he worshipped before Him. He and Eve worshipped Him and gave Him thanks because He had dealt mercifully with them. 5 Then God commanded the three angels, Michael, Gabriel and Raphael each to bring what he had brought and give it to Adam. And they did so, one by one. 6 And God commanded Suriyel and Salathiel to bear up Adam and Eve, and bring them down from the top of the high mountain, and to take them to the Cave of Treasures. 7 There they laid the gold on the south side of the cave, the incense on the eastern side, and the myrrh on the western side. For the mouth of the cave was on the north side. 8 The angels then comforted Adam and Eve, and departed. 9 The gold was seventy rods. The incense was twelve pounds, and the myrrh was three pounds. 10 These remained by Adam in the Cave of

Treasures, in the House of Treasures; therefore was it called 'Cave of Concealment.' And it was called the 'Cave of Treasures,' by reason of the bodies of righteous men that were in it. 11 God gave these three things to Adam on the third day after he had come out of the garden as a sign of the three days the Lord should remain in the heart of the earth. 12 And these three things, as they continued with Adam in the cave, gave him light by night, and by day they gave him a little relief from his sorrow.

Author's note: A rod is a unit of linear measure equal to approximately 5.5 yards and also a unit of area measure equivalent to approximately 30.25 square yards. Rod is also a description indicating a long, thin piece of unspecified size.

Author's note: Suriyel means "Command of God" and is one of the archangels from Judaic traditions. Other possible versions of his name are Suriel, Suriyel,(Some Dead Sea Scrolls translations), Esdreel, Sahariel, Juriel, Seriel, Sauriel, Surya, Jariel. The angel is mentioned in the Lost Book Of Enoch.
Salathiel means, "Whom I asked of God." The name is the son of Jeconiah (Matt. 1:12; 1 Chr. 3:17); also called the son of Neri (Luke 3:27) The probable explanation of the apparent discrepancy is that he was the son of Neri, the descendant of Nathan, and thus heir to the throne of David on the death of Jeconiah . See Jer. 22:30). The name acknowledges that the son is an answer to the parents' prayer to God (El) to help them conceive and birth a child. In 2 Esdras, the author claims to be "Ezra, who is also called

Shealtiel" (3:1). For this reason, this work is also sometimes known as Ezra Shealtiel.

Chapter XXXII

1 And Adam and Eve remained in the Cave of Treasures until the seventh day. They neither ate of the fruit of the earth, nor drank water. 2 And on the eighth day, when it dawned, Adam said to Eve, " Eve, we prayed God to give us something from the garden and He sent his angels who brought us what we had desired. 3 But now, get up, and let us go to the sea of water we saw at first, and let us stand in it and pray that God will again be favorable to us and take us back to the garden, or give us something, or that He will give us comfort in some other land than this one we are in." 4 Then Adam and Eve came out of the cave and went and stood on the border of the sea in which they had thrown themselves before. 5 Then Adam said to Eve: "Come, go down into this place, and do not come out until the end of thirty days, when I shall come to you. And pray to God with burning heart and a sweet voice to forgive us. 6 And I will go to another place, and go down into it and do like you." 7 Then Eve went down into the water as Adam had commanded her. Adam also went down into the water, and they stood praying, and besought the Lord to forgive them their offense and to restore them to their former state. 8 And they stood like that praying until the end of the thirty-five days.

Author's note: There is a discrepancy between the 30 days mentioned first and the 35 days cited later in the chapter. The number 35 is a combination of 3, the number of spiritual completion, and 5, the number of grace.

Chapter XXXIII

1 But Satan, the hater of all that is good, sought them in the cave, but did not find them although he searched diligently for them. 2 But he found them standing in the water praying and thought within himself, "Adam and Eve are standing like that in that water praying to God to forgive them their transgression, and to restore them to their former state, and to take them from under my hand. 3 But I will deceive them so that they shall come out of the water, and not fulfill their vow." 4 Then the hater of all that is good, did not go to Adam, but he went to Eve, and took the form of an angel of God, praising and rejoicing, and he said to her: 5 "Peace be to you! Be glad and rejoice! God is favorable to you and He sent me to Adam. I have brought him the glad tidings of salvation and of his being filled with bright light as he was at first. 6 And Adam, in his joy for his restoration, has sent me to you so that you would come with me in order that I might crown you with light like him. 7 And he said to me, 'Speak to Eve; if she does not come with you, tell her of the sign when we were on the top of the mountain, how God sent his angels who took us and brought us to the Cave of Treasures; and laid the gold on the southern side, incense on the eastern side, and myrrh on the western side.' Now come to him." 8 When Eve heard these words from him, she rejoiced much. And thinking Satan's appearance was

real; she came out of the sea. 9 He went first and she followed him until they came to Adam. Then Satan hid himself from her and she saw him no more. 10 She then came and stood before Adam, who was standing by the water and she rejoiced in God's forgiveness. 11 And as she called to him, he turned around and found her there and cried when he saw her and beat his chest from the bitterness of his grief. He sank into the water. 12 But God looked at him and at his misery and that he was about to breathe his last breath. And the Word of God came from heaven, raised him out of the water, and said to him, "Go up the high bank to Eve." And when he came up to Eve he said to her, "Who told you to come here?" 13 Then she told him the discourse of the angel who had appeared to her and had given her a sign. 14 But Adam grieved, and explained to her that it was Satan. He then took her and they both returned to the cave. 15 These things happened to them the second time they went down to the water seven days after their coming out of the garden. 16 They fasted in the water thirty-five days. It was altogether forty-two days since they had left the garden.

Chapter XXXIV

1 On the morning of the forty-third day, they came out of the cave, sorrowful and crying. Their bodies were lean, and they were parched from hunger and thirst, from fasting and praying, and from their heavy sorrow because of their transgression. 2 And when they had come out of the cave they went up the mountain to the west of the

garden. 3 There they stood and prayed and asked God to grant them forgiveness of their sins. 4 And after their prayers Adam began to beg God, saying, "O my Lord, my God, and my Creator, You commanded the four elements to be gathered together, and they were gathered together by Your order. 5 Then You spread Your hand and created me out of one element, that of dust of the earth. You brought me into the garden at the third hour, on a Friday, and informed me of it in the cave. 6 Then, at first, I knew neither night nor day, because I had a bright nature so that the light in which I lived ever left me to know night or day. 7 Then, again, O Lord, in that third hour in which You created me, You brought to me all beasts, and lions, and ostriches, and fowls of the air, and all things that move in the earth, which You had created at the first hour before me of the Friday. 8 And Your will was that I should name them all, one by one, with a suitable name. But You gave me understanding and knowledge and a pure heart and a right mind from you, that I should name them after Your own mind regarding the naming of them. 9 O God, You made them obedient to me and ordered that not one of them break from my control according to Your commandment and to the dominion which You had given me over them. But now they are all estranged from me. 10 Then it was in that third hour of Friday, in which You created me, and commanded me concerning the tree, to which I was neither to go near, nor to eat from; because You said to me in the garden, 'When you eat of it, from death you shall die.' 11 But if You had punished me as You said, with death, I should have died that very moment. 12 When You commanded me regarding the tree, that I was neither to approach nor to eat of it, Eve was not with me. You had not yet created her, neither had You yet taken her out of my side, so had she yet heard this order from you. 13 Then, at the end of the third hour of that Friday, O Lord, You caused a sleep to come over me, and I slept, and was overwhelmed in sleep. 14 Then You took a rib out of my side and You created her after my own likeness and image. Then I awoke and when I saw her and knew who she was, I said, 'This is bone of my bones, and flesh of my flesh. From now on she shall be called woman.' 15 It was of Your good will, O God, that You brought a sleep over me and that You quickly drew Eve out of my side until she was fully out, so that I did not see how she was made, neither could I witness. O my Lord, Your goodness and glory are awful and great. 16 And of Your goodwill, O Lord, You made us both with bodies of a bright nature, and You made the two of us one. You gave us Your grace and filled us with praises of the Holy Spirit that we should be neither hungry nor thirsty nor know what sorrow is, nor know faintness of heart, neither suffering, fasting nor weariness. 17 But now, O God, since we transgressed Your commandment and broke Your law, You have brought us out into a strange land, and have caused suffering, faintness, hunger and thirst to come over us. 18 Now, therefore, O God, we pray you, give us something to eat from the garden, to satisfy our hunger with it, and something wherewith to quench our thirst. 19 For, behold, many days, O God, we have tasted nothing and drunk nothing, and our flesh has dried up and our strength is wasted. Sleep is gone from our eyes from faintness and crying. 20 Then, O God, we dare not gather anything from the fruit of trees, from fear of you. For when we transgress the first time You spared us and did not make us die. 21 But now, we thought in our hearts that if we eat the fruit of the trees without God's order He will destroy us this time and will remove us from the earth. 22 And if we drink of this water without God's order He will make an end of us and root us up at once. 23 Now, therefore, O God, I have come to this place with Eve, and we beg You to give us some fruit from the garden so that we may be satisfied with it. 24 For we desire the fruit that is on the earth and all else that we lack in it."

Author's note: The four elements referred to are earth, air, fire, and water. Man was formed from dust, or earth.

Chapter XXXV

1 Then God looked again at Adam and his crying and groaning, and the Word of God came to him, and said to him: 2 "Adam, when you were in My garden, you knew neither eating nor drinking, faintness nor suffering, leanness of flesh, nor change; neither did sleep depart from your eyes. But since you transgressed and came into this strange land all these trials have come over you."

Author's note: It is unclear as to if this implies that Adam did not sleep or if he had no trouble sleeping while in the garden. Other verses seem to hint at the fact that his "bright nature and the perpetual glory of God shining in the garden provided no need nor place for sleep. While in the garden, Adam may not have needed sleep.

Chapter XXXVI

1 Then God commanded the cherub, who guarded the gate of the garden with a sword of fire in his hand, to take some of the fruit of the fig-tree and to give it to Adam. 2 The cherub obeyed the command of the Lord God and went into the garden and brought two figs on two twigs, each fig hanging to its leaf. They were from two of the trees among which Adam and Eve hid themselves when God went to walk in the garden and the Word of God came to Adam and Eve and said to them, "Adam! Adam! Where are you?" 3 And Adam answered, "O God, here I am. When I heard the sound of You and Your voice, I hid myself, because I am naked." 4 Then the cherub took two figs and brought them to Adam and Eve. But he threw the figs to them from a distance because they would not come near the cherub, for their flesh that could not come near the fire. 5 At first, angels trembled at the presence of Adam and were afraid of him. But now Adam trembled before the angels and was afraid of them. 6 Then Adam came closer and took one fig, and Eve also came in turn and took the other. 7 And as they took them up in their hands they looked at them and knew they were from the trees among which they had hidden themselves.

Chapter XXXVII

1 Then Adam said to Eve, "Do you not see these figs and their leaves with which we covered ourselves when we were stripped of our bright nature? But now, we do not know what misery and suffering may come to us from eating them. 2 Now, therefore, Eve, let us restrain ourselves and not eat them. Let us ask God to give us of the fruit of the Tree of Life." 3 So Adam and Eve restrained themselves and did not eat these figs. 4 But Adam began to pray to God and to beg Him to give him of the fruit of the Tree of Life, saying: "O God, when we transgressed Your commandment at the sixth hour of Friday, we were stripped of the bright nature we had, and did not continue in the garden after our transgression more than three hours. 5 But in the evening You made us come out of it. O God, we transgressed against You one hour and all these trials and sorrows have come over us until this day. 6 And those days together with this the forty-third days do not redeem that one hour in which we transgressed! 7 O God, look at us with an eye of pity, and do not avenge us according to our transgression of Your commandment in Your presence. 8 O God, give us of the fruit of the Tree of Life that we may eat it and live and turn not to see sufferings and other trouble in this earth, for You are God. 9 When we transgressed Your commandment You made us come out of the garden and sent a cherub to keep the Tree of Life so that we should not eat thereof and live and know nothing of faintness after we transgressed. 10 But

now, O Lord, behold, we have endured all these days and have borne sufferings. Make these forty-three days an equivalent for the one hour in which we transgressed."

Author's note: The day begins at sundown, or about 6 P.M. This would mean that is the sin occurred in the sixth hour it would have been midnight in the garden. If Adam and Eve were removed three hours afterward it would have been 3 A.M.

Chapter XXXVIII

1 After these things the Word of God came to Adam, and said to him: 2 "Adam, as to the fruit on the Tree of Life that you have asked for, I will not give it to you now, but only when the 5,500 years are fulfilled. At that time I will give you fruit from the Tree of Life and you will eat and live forever, both you and Eve, and also your righteous descendants. 3 But these forty-three days cannot make amends for the hour in which you transgressed My commandment. 4 Adam, I gave you the fruit of the fig-tree in which you hid yourself for you to eat. So, you and Eve go and eat it. 5 I will not deny your request; neither will I disappoint your hope. Therefore, endure until the fulfillment of the covenant I made with you." 6 And God withdrew His Word from Adam.

Chapter XXXIX

1 Then Adam returned to Eve and said to her, "Get up, and take a fig for yourself, and I will take the other; and let us go to our cave." 2 Then Adam and Eve each took a fig and went toward the cave. The time was about the setting of the sun and their thoughts made them long to eat of the fruit. 3 But Adam said to Eve, "I am afraid to eat of this fig. I do not know what may come over me from it." 4 So Adam cried and stood praying before God saying, "Satisfy my hunger, without my having to eat this fig because after I have eaten it, what will it profit me? And what shall I desire and ask of you, O God, when it is gone?" 5 And he said again, "I am afraid to eat of it; for I do not know what will befall me through it."

Chapter XL

1 Then the Word of God came to Adam and said to him, "Adam, why didn't you have this trepidation, or this will to fast, or this care before now? And why didn't you have this fear before you transgressed? 2 But when you came to live in this strange land your animal body could not survive on earth without earthly food to strengthen it and to restore its powers." 3 And God withdrew His Word for Adam.

Chapter XLI

1 Then Adam took the fig and laid it on the golden rods. Eve also took her fig and put it on the incense. 2 And the weight of each fig was that of a water-melon; for the fruit of the garden was much larger than the fruit of this land. 3 But Adam and Eve remained standing and fasting the entirety of that night until the morning dawned. 4 When the sun rose they were still praying, but after they had finished praying Adam said to Eve: 5 "Eve, come, let us go to the border of the garden looking south to the place from where the river flows and is parted into four heads. There we will pray to God and ask Him to give us some of the Water of Life to drink. 6 For God has not fed us with the Tree of Life in order that we may not live. Therefore, we will ask him to give us some of the Water of Life to quench our thirst with it, rather than with a drink of water of this land." 7 When Eve heard these words from Adam she agreed, and they both got up and came to the southern border of the garden, at the edge of the river of water a short distance from the garden. 8 And they stood and prayed before the Lord, and asked Him to look at them and for this one time to forgive them, and to grant them their request. 9 After this prayer from both of them, Adam began to pray with his voice before God, and said; 10 "O Lord, when I was in the garden and saw the water that flowed from under the Tree of Life, my heart did not desire, neither did my body require to drink of it. I did not know thirst, because I was living, and above that which I am

now. 11 So that in order to live I did not require any Food of Life nor did I need to drink of the Water of Life. 12 But now, O God, I am dead and my flesh is parched with thirst. Give me of the Water of Life that I may drink of it and live. 13 O God, through Your mercy save me from these plagues and trials, and bring me into another land different from this. Let me live in Your garden."

Author's note: One could extrapolate the size of the fruit, knowing that the size of the fig leaves were large enough to fashion loincloths from them. (See Genesis 3:7) Later, we are told the size of a fig was that of a watermelon.

Chapter XLII

1 Then the Word of God came to Adam, and said to him: 2 "Adam, you said, 'Bring me into a land where there is rest.' Another land than this will not bring you rest. It is the kingdom of heaven alone where there is rest. 3 But you cannot enter into it at present, but only after your judgment is past and fulfilled. 4 Then will I make you go up into the kingdom of heaven, you and your righteous descendants; and I will give you and them the rest you ask for now. 5 And if you said, 'Give me of the Water of Life that I may drink and live,' it cannot be this day, but on the day that I shall descend into hell, and break the gates of brass, and crush into pieces the kingdoms of iron. 6 Then I will, through mercy, save your soul and the souls of the righteous, and thus give them rest in My garden. That shall be when the end of the world is come. 7 And the Water of Life you seek will

not be granted you this day, but on the day that I shall shed My blood on your head in the land of Golgotha. 8 For My blood shall be the Water of Life to you at that time, and not to just you alone but to all your descendants who shall believe in Me. This will be rest to them for forever." 9 The Lord said again to Adam, "Adam, when you were in the garden these trials did not come to you. 10 But since you transgressed My commandment, all these sufferings have covered you. 11 Now, also, your flesh requires food and drink. So drink then of that water that flows by you on the face of the earth. 12 Then God withdrew His Word from Adam. 13 And Adam and Eve worshipped the Lord, and returned from the river of water to the cave. It was noon when they drew near to the cave, they saw a large fire by it.

Author's note: The kingdom of iron refers to Rome.
Jesus was fixed to the cross above the ground and the people, (raised up so that all would be brought to Him) and the blood flowed from above and fell on the people below on Golgotha (goal-goth-uh), which was the hill outside the walls of Jerusalem where Jesus was crucified. See John 6:25 and 7:38

Chapter XLIII

1 Then Adam and Eve were afraid, and stood still. And Adam said to Eve, "What is that fire by our cave? We have done nothing in it to cause this fire. 2 We neither have bread to bake, nor broth to cook there. We have never known anything like this fire, and we do not know what to call it. 3 But ever since God sent the cherub with a

sword of fire that flashed in his hand and had lightning coming from it we fell down and were like corpses from fear and we have not seen the like. 4 But now, Eve, look, this is the same fire that was in the cherub's hand, which God has sent to keep the cave in which we live. 5 O Eve, it is because God is angry with us and will drive us from it. 6 Eve, we have transgressed His commandment again in that cave, so that He had sent this fire to burn around it and prevent us from going into it. 7 If this is really the case, Eve, where shall we live? And where shall we flee to be away from the face of the Lord? Since, like it is with the garden, He will not let us live in it, and He has deprived us of the good things of it. But He has placed us in this cave, in which we have endured darkness, tests and hardships until at last we have found comfort in it. 8 But now that He has brought us out into another land, who knows what may happen in it? And who knows but that the darkness of that land may be far greater than the darkness of this land? 9 Who knows what may happen in that land by day or by night? And who knows whether it will be far or near, Eve? Do you think it will please God to put us far from the garden, Eve? Where will God put us to prevent us from beholding Him, because we have transgressed His commandment, and because we have made requests of Him all the time? 10 Eve, if God will bring us into a strange land other than this, in which we find consolation, it must be to put our souls to death, and blot out our name from the face of the earth. 11 O Eve, if we are further alienated from the garden and from God, where shall we find Him again, and ask Him to give us gold, incense, myrrh, and some fruit of the fig-tree? 12

Where shall we find Him to comfort us a second time? Where shall we find Him so that He may think of us regarding the covenant He has made on our behalf?" 13 Then Adam said nothing else more. And they kept looking, he and Eve, towards the cave, and at the fire that flared up around it. 14 But that fire was from Satan. For he had gathered trees and dry grasses, and had carried and brought them to the cave, and had set fire to them, in order to consume the cave and what was in it. 15 So that Adam and Eve should be left in sorrow, and he should cut off their trust in God, and make them deny Him. 16 But by the mercy of God he could not burn the cave because God sent His angel to the cave to guard it from this fire, until it went out. 17 And this fire lasted from noon until the break of the next day. That was the forty-fifth day.

Chapter XLIV

1 Adam and Eve stood, looking at the fire and were unable to come near the cave from their fear of the fire. 2 And Satan kept on bringing trees and throwing them into the fire until the flames of the fire rose up very high and covered the entire cave, thinking in his mind, to consume the cave with the great fire. But the angel of the Lord was guarding it. 3 But he could not curse Satan nor wound him by word because he had no authority over him, neither did he attempt to do so with words from his mouth. 4 Therefore the angel tolerated him without uttering a bad word against him, until the Word of God came to Satan saying, "Go away from here at once before you deceive

My servants, for this time you seek to destroy them. 5 Were it not for My mercy I would have destroyed you and your hosts from off the earth. But I have had patience with you until the end of the world." 6 Then Satan fled from before the Lord. But the fire went on burning around the cave like a coal-fire the entire day. This was the forty-sixth day that Adam and Eve had spent since they came out of the garden. 7 And when Adam and Eve saw that the heat of the fire had began to cool down, they started to walk toward the cave to get into it as they usually did but they could not because of the heat of the fire. 8 Then they both began crying because the fire separated them from the cave, and the fire came toward them, burning, and they were afraid. 9 Then Adam said to Eve, "See this fire of which we have a portion within us. It formerly obeyed us, but it no longer does so now, for we have violated the boundaries of creation and changed our condition and our nature has been altered. But the fire is not changed in its nature, nor altered from its creation. Therefore it now has power over us and when we come near it, it scorches our flesh."

Author's note: The Word of the Lord spoke to Satan stating, "I have had patience with you until the end of the world." This is a statement spoken in the future and recorded in the past. The precise meaning indicates that the statement was made at or after the end of the world.

Chapter XLV

1 Then Adam rose and prayed to God, saying, "This fire has

separated us from the cave in which You have commanded us to live; and now, we cannot go into it." 2 Then God heard Adam, and sent him His Word, that said: 3 "Adam, see this fire! It is different from the flame and heat from the garden of delights and the good things in it! 4 When you were under My control all creatures yielded to you, but after you transgressed My commandment they all rose up over you." 5 God said again to him, "Adam, see how Satan has exalted you! He has deprived you of the Godhead and of an exalted state like Me, and has not kept his word to you but has ended up to become your enemy. He is the one who made this fire in which he meant to burn you and Eve. 6 Adam, why has he not kept his agreement with you even one day, but has deprived you of the glory that was on you when you obeyed his command? 7 Adam, do you think that he loved you when he made this agreement with you? Do you think that he loved you and wished to raise you on high? 8 No, Adam, he did not do anything out of love for you. He wished to force you to come out of light and into darkness, and from an exalted state to degradation, and from glory to this humble state, from joy to sorrow, and from rest to hunger and fainting." 9 God also said to Adam, "See this fire kindled by Satan around your cave? See this curious thing that surrounds you? Know that it will surround both you and your descendants when you obey his command and he will plague you with fire and you will go down into hell after you are dead. 10 Then, you will experience the burning of his fire that will surround you and your descendants. You will not be delivered from it until My coming. Just as you cannot go into your cave right now because of the great fire around it, a way for you will not be made for you until My Word comes on the day My covenant is fulfilled. 11 There is no way for you at present to come from this life to rest until he who is My Word comes. Then He will make a way for you, and you shall have rest." Then God called to the fire that burned around the cave with His Word, that it split itself in half until Adam passed through it. Then the fire parted itself by God's order and a way was made for Adam. 12 And God withdrew His Word from Adam.

Author's note: By God's word His servants passed through the fire, just as the waters were parted.
The "WORD" is made flesh in the form of the Messiah.

Chapter XLVI

1 Then Adam and Eve began again to come into the cave. And when they came to the passage in the midst of the fire, Satan blew into the fire like a whirlwind and caused the burning coal-fire to cover Adam and Eve so that their bodies were singed and the coal-fire burned their skin. 2 Adam and Eve screamed from the burning of the fire, and said, "O Lord, save us! Do not leave us to be consumed and plagued by this burning fire. Do not require us as the payment for having transgressed Your commandment." 3 Then God looked at their bodies on which Satan had caused fire to burn. God sent His angel that held back the burning fire. But the wounds remained on their bodies. 4 Then God said to Adam, "See Satan's love for you. He

pretended to give you the Godhead and greatness and, now look, he burns you with fire and seeks to destroy you from off the earth. 5 Then look at Me, Adam. I created you, and how many times have I delivered you out of his hand? If not, wouldn't he have destroyed you?" 6 God spoke again, this time to Eve and said, "He promised you in the garden, saying, 'As soon as you eat from the tree, your eyes will be opened, and you shall become like gods, knowing good and evil.' But look! He has burned your bodies with fire and has made you taste the taste of fire, in exchange for the taste of the garden. He has made you see the burning of fire, and the evil of it, and the power it has over you. 7 Your eyes have seen the good he has taken from you, and in truth he has opened your eyes. You have seen the garden in which you were with Me, and you have also seen the evil that has come over you from Satan. But as to the, Godhead he cannot give it to you, nor fulfill his promise to you. He was bitter against you and your descendants, that will come after you." 8 And God withdrew His Word form them.

Chapter XLVII

1 Then Adam and Eve came into the cave, still trembling because of the fire that had scorched them. So Adam said to Eve: 2 "Look, in this world the fire burns our flesh. How will it be when we are dead and Satan shall punish our souls? Is not our deliverance far off unless God comes in His mercy and fulfills His promise to us?" 3 Then Adam and Eve stepped into the cave blessing themselves for coming

into it once more. For they thought that they would never enter it, when they saw the fire around it. 4 But as the sun was setting the fire was still burning and coming closer to Adam and Eve in the cave, so that they could not sleep in it. After the sunset they went out of the cave. This was the forty-seventh day after they came out of the garden. 5 Adam and Eve then came under the top of hill by the garden to sleep, as they were accustomed. 6 And they stood and prayed God to forgive them their sins, and then fell asleep under the top of the mountain. 7 But Satan, the hater of all that is good, thought to himself: "God has promised salvation to Adam by covenant, and promised that He would deliver him from all the hardships that have befallen him, but God has not promised me by covenant, and will not deliver me out of my hardships. He has promised Adam that He should make him and his descendants live in the kingdom that I once lived in. I will kill Adam. 8 The earth shall be rid of him. The earth shall be left to me alone. When he is dead he will not have any descendants left to inherit the kingdom and it will remain my own realm. God will then be wanting me, and He will restore it to me and my hosts."

Chapter XLVIII

1 After this Satan called to his hosts, all of which came to him, and said to him: 2 "Our lord, what will you do?" 3 Then he said to them, "This Adam, whom God created out of the dust, is the one who has taken our kingdom from us. Come, let us gather together and kill

him. Hurl a rock at him and at Eve, and crush them under it." 4
When Satan's hosts heard these words they came to the part of the
mountain where Adam and Eve were asleep. 5 Then Satan and his
host took a huge rock, broad and smooth, and without blemish. He
thought to himself, "If there should be a hole in the rock, when it fell
on them the hole in the rock might align over them so they would
escape and not die." 6 He then said to his hosts, "Take up this stone
and drop it flat on them so that it doesn't roll off them to somewhere
else. And when you have hurled it at them get away from there
quickly." 7 And they did as he told them. But as the rock fell down
from the mountain toward Adam and Eve, God commanded the rock
to become a covering over them so that it did them no harm. And so
it was by God's order. 8 But when the rock fell, the whole earth
quaked because of it, and was shaken from the size of the rock. 9
And as it quaked and shook Adam and Eve awoke from sleep and
found themselves under a covering of rock. But they didn't know
what had happened because when they fell asleep they were under
the sky and not under a covering, and when they saw it they were
afraid. 10 Then Adam said to Eve, "How has the mountain bent itself
and the earth quaked and shaken on our account? And why has this
rock spread itself over us like a tent? 11 Does God intend to plague
us and to shut us up in this prison? Or will He close the earth over
us? 12 He is angry with us for our having come out of the cave
without His permission and for our having done so of our own
accord without asking Him when we left the cave and came to this
place." 13 Then Eve said, "Adam, if indeed the earth shook for our

sake and this rock formed a tent over us because of our transgression we will be sorry, because our punishment will be long. 14 But get up and pray to God to let us know concerning this, and what this rock is that is spread over us like a tent." 15 Then Adam stood up and prayed before the Lord to let him know what had brought about this difficult time. And Adam stood praying like that until the morning.

Chapter XLIX

1 Then the Word of God came and said: 2 "O Adam, who counseled you when you came out of the cave to come to this place?" 3 And Adam said to God, "Lord, we came to this place because of the heat of the fire that came over us inside the cave." 4 Then the Lord God said to Adam, "Adam, you dread the heat of fire for one night, but how will it be when you live in hell? 5 But Adam, do not be afraid and do not believe that I have placed this covering of rock over you to plague you. 6 It came from Satan, who had promised you the Godhead and majesty. It is he who threw down this rock to kill you under it, and Eve with you, and in this way to prevent you from living on the earth. 7 But, as that rock was falling down on you I was merciful. I commanded it to form a tent over you, and the rock under you to lower itself. 8 And this sign, O Adam, will happen to Me at My coming on earth: Satan will raise the people of the Jews to put Me to death and they will lay Me in a rock, and seal a large stone over Me, and I shall remain within that rock three days and three nights. 9 But on the third day I shall rise again, and it shall be salvation to you,

O Adam, and to your descendants, so that you will believe in Me. But, Adam, I will not bring you from under this rock until three days and three nights have passed." 10 And God withdrew His Word from Adam. 11 But Adam and Eve lived under the rock three days and three nights, as God had told them. 12 And God did so to them because they had left their cave and had come to this same place without God's permission. 13 But, after three days and three nights, God created an opening in the covering of rock and allowed them to get out from under it. Their flesh was dried up, and their eyes and hearts were troubled from crying and sorrow.

Author's note: Some translations have the rock forming a dome, but the text gives no shape. If one reads the text closely, it becomes obvious that the shape of the falling rock may not be as important as the fact that the ground Adam and Eve were sleeping on was made to form a depression between the tent or dome shape and the depression of the ground. This formed a cave shape, which mimicked the cave in which Jesus would be buried. It is less obvious but implied that Adam and Eve had some amount of light inside the cave. The text gives no explanation, whether there were gaps, cracks, or holes for air and light.

Chapter L

1 Then Adam and Eve went out and came into the Cave of Treasures and stood praying in it the entire day until the evening. 2 And this

took place at the end of the fifty days after they had left the garden. 3 But Adam and Eve rose again and prayed to God in the cave the whole of that night, and begged for mercy from Him. 4 And when the day dawned, Adam said to Eve, "Come! Let us go and do some work for our bodies." 5 So they went out of the cave, and came to the northern border of the garden, and they looked for something to cover their bodies with. But they found nothing, and did not know how to do the work. But their bodies were stained, and they could not speak from cold and heat. 6 Then Adam stood and asked God to show him something with which to cover their bodies. 7 Then came the Word of God and said to him, "O Adam, take Eve and come to the seashore where you fasted before. There you will find skins of sheep that were left after lions ate the carcasses. Take them and make garments for yourselves, and clothe yourselves with them.

Author's Note: There is no direct explanation as to how Adam and Eve became naked again. One possibility is found in chapter XLVI, verse 1, which states that Satan blew into the fire and singed Adam and Eve. It is possible that the garments that the Lord had given them in Genesis 3:21 were burned away at this point, leaving Adam and Eve naked once more.

Chapter LI

1 When Adam heard these words from God, he took Eve and went from the northern side of the garden to the south of it, by the river of

water where they once fasted. 2 But as they were on their way, and before they arrived, Satan, the wicked one, had heard the Word of God communing with Adam respecting his covering. 3 It distressed him, and he hurried to the place where the sheepskins were, with the intention of taking them and throwing them into the sea or of burning them so that Adam and Eve would not find them. 4 But as he was about to take them, the Word of God came from heaven and bound him by the side of those skins until Adam and Eve came near him. But as they got closer to him they were afraid of him and of his hideous appearance. 5 Then the Word of God came to Adam and Eve, and said to them, "This is he who was hidden in the serpent, who deceived you, and stripped from you your garment of light and glory. 6 This is he who promised you majesty and divinity. Where is the beauty that was on him? Where is his divinity? Where is his light? Where is the glory that rested on him? 7 Now his form is hideous. He has become abominable (offensive) among angels, and he has come to be called Satan. 8 Adam, he wished to steal from you this earthly garment of sheepskins so that he could destroy it not let you be covered with it. 9 What is his beauty that you should have followed him? And what have you gained by obeying him? See his evil works and then look at Me, your Creator. Look at the good deeds I do for you. 10 I bound him until you came and saw him and his weakness and that no power is left with him." 11 And God released him from his bonds.

Chapter LII

1 After this Adam and Eve said no more, but cried before God because of their creation, and their bodies that required an earthly covering. 2 Then Adam said to Eve, "Eve, this is the skin of beasts with which we shall be covered, but when we put it on we shall be wearing a sign of death on our bodies. Just as the owners of these skins have died and have decomposed, so also shall we die and pass away." 3 Then Adam and Eve took the skins and went back to the Cave of Treasures. When they were in it, they stood and prayed, as was their habit. 4 And they thought how they could make garments of those skins because they had no skill. 5 Then God sent to them His angel to show them how to accomplish this. And the angel said to Adam, "Go out and bring some palm-thorns." Then Adam went out, and brought some, as the angel had commanded him. 6 Then the angel began before them to work the skins, after the manner of one who prepares a shirt. And he took the thorns and stuck them into the skins before their eyes. 7 Then the angel again stood up and prayed God that the thorns in those skins should be hidden, so as to be as if it were sewn with one thread. 8 And so it was, by God's order, and they became garments for Adam and Eve. And He clothed them with the skins. 9 From that time the nakedness of their bodies was covered from the sight of each other's eyes. 10 And this happened at the end of the fifty-first day. 11 Then when Adam's and Eve's bodies were covered they stood and prayed and sought mercy of the Lord and

forgiveness, and gave Him thanks because He had mercy on them and had covered their nakedness. And they did not stop praying the entirety of that night. 12 Then, when the morning dawned at sunrise, they said their prayers, as was their custom, and then went out of the cave. 13 And Adam said to Eve, "Since we don't know what there is to the west of this cave, let us go out and see it today." Then they departed and went toward the western border.

Chapter LIII

1 They were not very far from the cave when Satan came toward them. He hid himself between them and the cave in the form of two ravenous lions that had been three days without food. And they came toward Adam and Eve as if to break them in pieces and devour them. 2 Then Adam and Eve cried out and begged God to deliver them from their paws. 3 Then the Word of God came to them and drove away the lions from them. 4 And God said to Adam, "Adam, what do you seek on the western border? And why have you left of your own will the eastern border which was your living place? 5 Now, turn back to your cave and remain in it, so that Satan won't deceive you or achieve his goal to overtake you. 6 In this western border, Adam, there will go from you a descendant that shall replenish it. And they will defile themselves with their sins, and with their yielding to the commands of Satan, and by following his works. 7 Therefore will I bring waters of a flood to cover them and overwhelm them all. But I will deliver what is left of the righteous

among them and I will bring them to a distant land, but the land in which you live now shall remain desolate and without one inhabitant in it. 8 After God had spoken to them, they went back to the Cave of Treasures. But their flesh was dried up, and they were weak from fasting and praying, and from the sorrow they felt at having sinned against God.

Chapter LIV

1 Then Adam and Eve stood up in the cave and prayed the entire night until the morning dawned. And when the sun came up they both went out of the cave. Their minds were wandering from the heaviness of sorrow and they didn't know where they were going. 2 And they walked in that condition to the southern border of the garden. And they began to go up that border until they came to the eastern border, which was land's end. 3 And the cherub who guarded the garden was standing at the western gate to guard it from Adam and Eve in case they should attempt to suddenly come into the garden. 4 When Adam and Eve thought the cherub was not watching they came to the eastern border of the garden. But as they were standing by the gate, as if they desired to go in, the cherub turned around as if to put them to death according to the order God had given him. And the cherub suddenly came with a flashing sword of fire in his hand. When he saw them, he went toward them to kill them. For he was afraid that God would destroy him if they went into the garden without God's order. 5 And the sword of the cherub

seemed to shoot flames a distance away from it. But when he raised it over Adam and Eve, the flame of the sword did not flash out at them. 6 Because of this the cherub thought that God was approving to them and was bringing them back into the garden. And the cherub stood wondering. 7 He could not go up to Heaven to ascertain God's order regarding Adam and Eve's entering the garden so continued to stand by them, unable to leave them because he was afraid that if they should enter the garden without permission God would destroy him. 8 When Adam and Eve saw the cherub coming towards them with a flaming sword of fire in his hand they fell on their faces from fear, and were as dead. 9 Then, the heavens and the earth shook, and another cherubim came down from heaven to the cherub who guarded the garden, and saw him amazed and silent. 10 Then, again, other angels came down close to the place where Adam and Eve were. And the cherubs were split between joy and sorrow. 11 They were joyous because they thought that God was approving to Adam, and wished him to return to the garden and wished to return him to the gladness he once enjoyed. 12 But they were sorrowful over Adam because he was fallen like a dead man, he and Eve. And they said to themselves, "Adam has not died in this place, but God has put him to death for coming to this place and wishing to enter the garden without His permission."

Chapter LV

1 Then the Word of God came to Adam and Eve, and raised them up from their dead state, saying to them, "Why did you come up here? Do you intend to go into the garden from which I brought you out? You cannot return today but only when the covenant I have made with you is fulfilled." 2 Then Adam, when he heard the Word of God, and the fluttering of the angels, which he only heard and did not see, he and Eve cried and said to the angels: 3 "O Spirits, who wait on God, look at me and at my inability to see you! When I was in my former bright nature I could see you. I sang praises as you do and my heart was far above you. 4 But now that I have transgressed, that bright nature is gone from me and I have come to this miserable state in which I cannot see you. You do not serve me like you used to do. For my flesh has become like that of the animals. 5 O angels of God, ask God to restore me to the state I was in formerly and ask him to rescue me from this misery, and to remove the sentence of death He passed on me for having trespassed against Him. Ask Him, as I ask Him to do these things." 6 Then, when the angels heard these words they all grieved over him and cursed Satan who had misled Adam until he came from the garden to misery, and from life to death, and from peace to distress, and from gladness to a strange land. 7 Then the angels said to Adam, "You obeyed Satan and ignored the Word of God who created you. You believed that Satan would fulfill all he had promised you. 8 But now, Adam, we will make known to you what came over us though him, before his fall from heaven. 9 He

gathered together his hosts and deceived them, promising to give them a great kingdom, a divine nature, and other promises he made them. 10 His hosts believed that his word was true, so they followed him, and renounced the glory of God. 11 He then ordered us, and some obeyed and under his command, and accepted his empty promises. But we would not obey and we did not take his orders. 12 Then, after he had fought with God and had dealt disrespectfully with Him, he gathered together his hosts and made war with us. And if it had not been for God's strength that was with us we could not have prevailed against him to hurl him from heaven. 13 But when he fell from among us there was great joy in heaven because of his descent from us. If he had remained in heaven, nothing, not even one angel would have remained in it. 14 But God in His mercy drove him from among us to this dark earth because he had become darkness itself and a performer of unrighteousness. 15 And Adam, he has continued to make war against you until he tricked you and made you come out of the garden to this strange land, where all these trials have come to you. And death, which God brought to him, he has also brought to you because you obeyed him and sinned against God." 16 Then all the angels rejoiced and praised God and asked Him not to destroy Adam for his having sought to enter the garden at this time, but to bear with him until the fulfillment of the promise, and to help him in this world until he was free from Satan's hand.

Chapter LVI

1 Then the Word of God came to Adam, and said to him: 2 "Adam, look at that garden of joy and at this earth of toil, and see, the garden is full of angels, but look at yourself alone on this earth with Satan whom you obeyed. 3 If you had submitted and been obedient to Me and had kept My Word, you would be with My angels in My garden. 4 But when you sinned and obeyed Satan, you became his guests among his angels, that are full of wickedness, and you came to this earth that produces thorns and thistles for you. 5 O Adam, ask the one who deceived you to give you the divine nature he promised you, or to make you a garden as I had made for you, or to fill you with that same bright nature with which I had filled you. 6 Ask him to make you a body like the one I made you, or to give you a day of rest as I gave you, or to create within you a wise (intelligent, sound, reasonable) soul, as I created for you; or to take you from here to some other earth than this one which I gave you. But, Adam, he will not fulfill even one of the things he told you. 7 Acknowledge My favor toward you, and My mercy on you, My creature. Acknowledge that I have not shown vengeance on you for your transgression against Me, but in My pity for you I have promised you that at the end of the great five and a half days I will come and save you." 8 Then God said again to Adam and Eve, "Get up, go down from here before the cherub with a sword of fire in his hand destroys you." 9 But Adam's heart was comforted by God's words to him, and he worshipped before Him. 10 And God commanded His angels to

escort Adam and Eve to the cave with joy instead of the fear that had come over them. 11 Then the angels took up Adam and Eve and brought them down the mountain by the garden, with songs and praises and hymns until they arrived at the cave. There the angels began to comfort and to strengthen them, and then departed from them towards heaven to their Creator, who had sent them. 12 But after the angels had departed from Adam and Eve, Satan came with shamefacedness and stood at the entrance of the cave in which were Adam and Eve. He then called to Adam, and said, "O Adam, come, let me speak to you." 13 Then Adam came out of the cave, thinking he was one of God's angels that had come to give him some good counsel.

Chapter LVII

1 But when Adam came out and saw his hideous figure he was afraid of him, and said to him, "Who are you?" 2 Then Satan answered and said to him, "It is I, who hid myself within the serpent, and who spoke to Eve, and who enticed her until she obeyed my command. I am he who, using my deceitful speech, sent her to deceive you until you both ate of the fruit of the tree and rejected the command of God." 3 But when Adam heard these words from him, he said to him, "Can you make me a garden as God made for me? Or can you clothe me in the same bright nature in which God had clothed me? 4 Where is the divine nature you promised to give me? Where is that clever speech of yours that you had with us at first, when we were in the

garden?" 5 Then Satan said to Adam, "Do you think that when I have promised someone something that I would actually deliver it to him or fulfill my word? Of course not. I myself have no hope of (never even thought of) obtaining what I promised. 6 Therefore I fell, and I made you fall for the same reason that I myself fell. Whoever accepts my counsel, falls. 7 But now, O Adam, because you fell you are under my rule and I am king over you because you have obeyed me and have sinned against your God. There will be no deliverance from my hands until the day promised you by your God." 8 Again he said, "Because we do not know the day agreed on with you by your God, nor the hour in which you shall be delivered, we will multiply wars and murders on you and your descendants after you. 9 This is our will and our good pleasure that we may not leave one of the sons of men to inherit our place in heaven. 10 Our home, Adam, is in burning fire and we will not stop our evil doing even a single day nor even a single hour. And I, O Adam, shall set you on fire when you come into the cave to live there." 11 When Adam heard these words he cried and mourned and said to Eve, "Did you hear what he said? He said that he would not fulfill any of what he promised you in the garden. Did he really, at that time, become king over us? 12 We will ask God, who created us, to deliver us out of his hands."

Chapter LVIII

1 Then Adam and Eve spread their hands before God, praying and begging Him to drive Satan away from them so that he could not harm them or force them to deny God. 2 Then, suddenly, God sent to them His angel who drove Satan away from them. This happened about sunset on the fifty-third day after they had come out of the garden. 3 Then Adam and Eve went into the cave, and stood up and lowered their faces to the ground to pray to God. 4 But before they prayed Adam said to Eve, "Look, you have seen what temptations have befallen us in this land. Come, let us get up and ask God to forgive us the sins we have committed and we will not come out until the end of the day before the fortieth day. And if we die in here He will save us." 5 Then Adam and Eve got up and joined together in entreating God. 6 They continued praying like this in the cave and did not come out of it in the night or day, until their prayers went up out of their mouths like a flame of fire.

Author's note: This little chapter has several details showing connections to customs of punishment and also to number symbolism. The day is the 53rd day. 5+3=8. Eight is the number of judgment. Adam and Eve elected to stay in the cave praying for 40 days minus 1. Forty is the number of testing and trails. The rains were to fall for 40 days. Jesus was in the desert for 40 days. The Israelites wondered in the desert for 40 years… However, when it came to punishment inflicted by the state, as was in the case of the flogging of Jesus, the punishment was 40 lashes minus 1.

Chapter LIX

1 But Satan, the hater of all that is good, did not allow them to finish
their prayers. He called to his hosts and they all came. Then he said
to them, "Since Adam and Eve, whom we deceived, have agreed
together to pray to God night and day, and to beg Him to deliver
them, and since they will not come out of the cave until the end of
the fortieth day. 2 And since they will continue their prayers as they
have both agreed to do, that He will deliver them out of our hands
and restore them to their former state, let us see what we shall do to
them." And his hosts said to him, "Power is yours, our lord, to do
what you command." 3 Then Satan, great in wickedness, took his
hosts and came into the cave on the thirtieth night of the forty day
period, and he beat Adam and Eve until he thought they were dead
and he left them as dead. 4 Then the Word of God came to Adam and
Eve and raised them from their suffering, and God said to Adam, "Be
strong, and do not be afraid of him who has just come to you." 5 But
Adam cried and said, "Where were you, my God, that they should
punish me with such blows and that this suffering should come over
me and over Eve, your handmaiden?" 6 Then God said to him,
"Adam, see, he is lord and master of all you have, he who said, he
would give you divinity. Where is this love for you? And where is
the gift he promised? 7 Did it please him just once, Adam, to come to
you, comfort you, strengthen you, rejoice with you, or send his hosts
to protect you, because you have obeyed him and have obeyed his
counsel and have followed his commandment and transgressed

Mine?" 8 Then Adam cried before the Lord, and said, "Lord because I transgressed a little, You have severely punished me in return. I ask You to deliver me out of his hands, or at least have pity on me and take my soul out of my body now in this strange land." 9 Then God said to Adam, "If only there had been this moaning and praying before you transgressed you would have rest from the trouble in which you are now." 10 But God had patience with Adam, and let him and Eve remain in the cave until they had fulfilled the forty days. 11 But the strength and flesh withered on Adam and Eve from fasting and praying, from hunger and thirst, because they had not tasted either food or drink since they left the garden, and their bodies functioned erratically because they had no strength left to continue in prayer from hunger until the end of the next day to the fortieth. They were fallen down in the cave, yet what speech escaped from their mouths, was only in praises.

Chapter LX

1 Then on the eighty-ninth day, Satan came to the cave, clad in a garment of light, and belted with a bright girdle. 2 In his hands was a staff of light, and he looked most frightening, but his face was pleasant and his speech was sweet. 3 He had transformed himself like this in order to deceive Adam and Eve and to make them come out of the cave before they had fulfilled the forty days. 4 He said to himself, "When they had fulfilled the forty days' fasting and praying, God would restore them to their former state but if He did not do

this He would still be favorable to them, and even if He had no mercy on them would He still give them something from the garden to comfort them as He had already twice before." 5 Then Satan came near the cave in beautiful appearance and said: 6 "Adam, you and Eve arise and stand up and come along with me to a good land and don't be afraid. I am flesh and bones like you and at first I was a creature that God created. 7 It was like this when He had created me, He placed me in a garden in the north on the border of the world. 8 And He said to me, 'Stay here!' And I remained there according to His word and I did not violate His commandment. 9 Then He made a sleep to come over me and then He brought you, Adam, out of my side, but He did not make you stay with me. 10 But God took you in His holy hand and placed you in a garden to the east. 11 Then I worried about you, because even though God had taken you out of my side, He had not allowed you to stay with me. 12 But God said to me: 'Do not worry about Adam, whom I brought out of your side, no harm will come to him. 13 For now I have brought out of his side a help-meet for him and I have given him joy by so doing.' " 14 Then Satan spoke again, saying, "I did not know how it is you came to be in this cave, nor anything about this trial that has come over you until God said to me, 'Behold, Adam has transgressed. He whom I had taken out of your side, and Eve also, whom I took out of his side have sinned and I have driven them out of the garden. I have made them live in a land of sorrow and misery because they transgressed against Me, and have obeyed Satan. And look, they are suffering to this day, the eightieth.' 15 Then God said to me, 'Get up, go to them, and make them come to your place, and do not permit Satan to come near them and afflict them. For they are now in great misery and lie helpless from hunger.' 16 He further said to me, 'When you have taken them to yourself, give them to eat of the fruit of the Tree of Life and give them to drink of the water of peace, and clothe them in a garment of light, and restore them to their former state of grace, and leave them not in misery, for they came from you. But grieve not over them, nor be sorry of that which has come over them. 17 But when I heard this, I was sorry and my heart could not bear it for your sake and I could not wait, my child. 18 But, Adam, when I heard the name of Satan I was afraid, and I said to myself, I will not come out because he might trap me as he did my children, Adam and Eve. 19 And I said, 'God, when I go to my children, Satan will meet me on the way and fight against me as he did against them.' 20 Then God said to me, 'Fear not; when you find him, hit him with the staff that is in your hand and don't be afraid of him, because you are old and established, and he shall not prevail against you.' 21 Then I said, 'O my Lord, I am old, and cannot go. Send Your angels to bring them.' 22 But God said to me, 'Angels are not like Adam and Eve; and they will not consent to come with them. But I have chosen you, because they are your offspring and are like you and they will listen to what you say.' 23 God said further to me, 'If you don't have enough strength to walk, I will send a cloud to carry you and set you down at the entrance of their cave, then the cloud will return and leave you there. 24 And if they will come with you, I will send a cloud to carry you and them.' 25 Then He commanded a cloud to carry me up and it brought me to you, and then it went back. 26 And now, my children, Adam and Eve, look at my old gray hair and at my feeble state, and at my coming from that distant place. Come with me to a place of rest." 27 Then he began to cry and to sob before Adam and Eve, and his tears poured on the ground like water. 28 And when Adam and Eve raised their eyes and saw his beard and heard his sweet talk, their hearts softened towards him and they obeyed him, because they believed he was true. 29 And it seemed to them that they were really his offspring when they saw that his face was like their own; and they trusted him.

Author note: This chapter is a cruel mockery. It represents the purpose of Christ turned upside down. Satan claims to be sent by God because he is in human form, in order to rescued Adam and Eve because he was made like them and they would listen and obey him. Adam and Eve believed Satan. When Jesus came we rejected the true savior.

Later in the chapter the word "helpmeet" is used. Meet, in the archaic usage, means to be fit, suitable, or proper. Thus, in the King James usage, the word helpmeet means someone who is a fit or suitable helper. It was only in the 17th century that the two words help and meet were mistaken for one word, helpmeet, and came to mean a wife. Later, in the 18th century a mistake in spelling along with a misunderstanding of the broader meaning of the word produced the word "helpmate" to mean a wife or sexual mate.

Chapter LXI

1 Then Satan took Adam and Eve by the hand started to lead them out of the cave. 2 But when they had gone a little way out of it God knew that Satan had overcome them and had brought them out before the forty days were ended in order to take them to some distant place and to destroy them. 3 Then the Word of the Lord God again came and cursed Satan and drove him away from them. 4 And God began to speak to Adam and Eve, saying to them, "What made you come out of the cave to this place?" 5 Then Adam said to God, "Did you create a man before us? Because, when we were in the cave there suddenly came to us a friendly old man who said to us, 'I am a messenger from God to you, to bring you back to some place of rest.' 6 And we believed that he was a messenger from you, O God, and we came out with him. We did not know where we should go with him." 7 Then God said to Adam, "This is the father of the evil arts who brought you and Eve out of the Garden of Delights. And when he saw that you and Eve both joined together in fasting and praying so that you did not come out of the cave before the end of the forty days, he wished to make your efforts wasted and break your mutual bond in order to take away all hope from you and to drive you to some place where he might destroy you. 8 Because he couldn't do anything to you unless he showed himself in the likeness of you. 9 Therefore he came to you with a face like your own and began to give you signs as if they were all true. 10 But because I am merciful and am favorable to you, I did not allow him to destroy you. Instead,

I drove him away from you. 11 Now, Adam, take Eve and return to your cave and remain in it until the morning after the fortieth day. And when you come out, go toward the eastern gate of the garden." 12 Then Adam and Eve worshipped God, and praised and blessed Him for the deliverance that had come to them from Him. And they returned to the cave. This happened in the evening of the thirty-ninth day. 13 Then Adam and Eve stood up and with a fervent passion, prayed to God to give them strength, for they had become weak because of hunger and thirst and prayer. But they watched the entire night praying until morning. 14 Then Adam said to Eve, "Get up. Let us go toward the eastern gate of the garden as God told us." 15 And they said their prayers as they were accustomed to do every day, and they left the cave to go near to the eastern gate of the garden. 16 Then Adam and Eve stood up and prayed and appealed to God to strengthen them and to send them something to satisfy their hunger. 17 But after they finished their prayers they were too weak to move. 18 Then the Word of God came again, and said to them, "Adam, get up, go and bring the two figs here." 19 Then Adam and Eve got up, and went until they came near to the cave.

Chapter LXII

1 But Satan, the wicked one, was envious because of the consolation God had given them. 2 So he prevented them from getting the figs and went into the cave and took the two figs and buried them outside the cave so that Adam and Eve should not find them. He also

had thought to destroy them. 3 But by God's mercy, as soon as those two figs were in the ground God defeated Satan's wishes regarding the figs and made them into two fruit trees that grew higher than the cave and shaded the cave because Satan had buried them on the eastern side of it. 4 Then when the two trees were grown, and were covered with fruit, Satan grieved and mourned, and said, "It would have been better to have left those figs where they were, because now they have become two fruit trees that Adam will eat from all the days of his life. But I had in my mind that when I buried them it would destroy them entirely and hide them forever. 5 But God has overturned my plan and would not let that sacred fruit perish, and He has made known my intention, and has defeated the plan I had formed against His servants." 6 Then Satan went away ashamed because he hadn't thought his plans all the way through.

Chapter LXIII

1 As they got closer to the cave Adam and Eve saw two fig trees covered with fruit, and giving shade to the cave. 2 Then Adam said to Eve, "It seems to me that we have gone the wrong way. When did these two trees grow here? It seems to me that the enemy wishes to lead us the wrong way. Do you suppose that there is another cave in the earth besides this one? 3 But, Eve let us go into the cave and find the two figs because this is our cave we were in. But if we do not find the two figs in it then it cannot be our cave." 4 Then they went into the cave and looked into the four corners of it but did not find the

two figs. 5 And Adam cried and said to Eve, "Did we go to the wrong cave, Eve? It seems to me the two figs should have been in the cave." And Eve said, "I, do not know." 6 Then Adam stood up and prayed and said, "O God, You commanded us to come back to the cave to take the two figs and return to you. 7 But now, we cannot find them. God, have you taken them and planted these two trees, or have we lost our way (gotten lost) in the earth, or has the enemy deceived us? If this is real then, O God, reveal the secret of these two trees (outside) and figs to us." 8 Then the Word of God came to Adam, and said to him, "Adam, when I sent you to bring back the figs, Satan went ahead of you to the cave and took the figs, and buried them outside, east of the cave, thinking to destroy them, by not sowing them with good intent. 9 It wasn't because of him that these trees have immediately grown up but I had mercy on you and I commanded them to grow. And they grew to be two large trees, that would give you shade by their branches, and you should find rest, and by this I made you see My power and My marvelous works. 10 And, also I showed you Satan's cruelty and his evil works. Ever since you came out of the garden he has not ceased for a single day from doing you harm in some way. But I have not given him power over you." 11 And God said, "From now on, Adam, rejoice because of the trees that you and Eve can rest under when you feel weary. But do not eat any of their fruit or come near them." 12 Then Adam cried, and said, "God, will You kill us again, or will You drive us away from Your face, and cut off our life from the face of the earth? 13 O God, I beg you, if You know that these trees bring either death or some other evil, as they did the first time, root them up from near our cave and leave us to die of the heat or hunger or thirst. 14 For we know Your marvelous works, O God, that they are great, and that by Your power You can bring one thing out of another without the thing's (person's) consent. For Your power can make rocks to become trees, and trees to become rocks."

Author's Note: They would have known it was their cave because the gold was still there. This verse brings up questions of Satan's power over Adam and Eve and the extent of any authority. In previous verses we were led to think Satan had gained power of them because of their sin. Now, in this verse we read," But I have not given him power over you." This seems to be a contradiction.

Chapter LXIV

1 Then God looked at Adam and at his strength of mind and at his ability to endure hunger, thirst, and heat. And He changed the two fig trees into two figs as they were at first. Then He said to Adam and Eve, "Each of you may take one fig." And they took them as the Lord commanded them. 2 And He said to them, "You must now go into the cave and eat the figs and satisfy your hunger or else you will die." 3 So, they went into the cave about sunset as God commanded them. And Adam and Eve stood up and prayed during the setting sun. 4 Then they sat down to eat the figs, but they did not know how to eat them because they were not accustomed to eating earthly food. They

were afraid that if they ate, their stomach would become heavy and their flesh thickened, and their hearts would begin to crave earthly food. 5 But while they were seated, God sent them His angel, out of pity for them, so they wouldn't perish of hunger and thirst. 6 And the angel said to Adam and Eve, "God says to you that you do not have the strength that would be required to fast until death, so eat and strengthen your bodies, for you are now animal flesh and cannot subsist without food and drink." 7 Then Adam and Eve took the figs and began to eat of them. But God had put into them a mixture as of savory bread and blood. 8 Then, the angel left Adam and Eve as they ate of the figs until they had satisfied their hunger. Then they put aside what was left over, but by the power of God the figs became whole again, because God blessed them. 9 After this Adam and Eve got up and prayed with a joyful heart and renewed strength, and praised and rejoiced much for the entire night. And this was the end of the eighty-third day.

Author's not: The meaning of the phrase, "God says to you that you do not have the strength that would be required to fast until death..." is not clear. It is likely that it simply is somewhat inverted and should be, "If you fast, you will not have the required strength and you will die." Although one could look at it as a spiritual strength and a warning the one does not have the required determination to endure death by fasting. But God saw Adam had the will.

Chapter LXV

1 And when it was day, they got up and prayed, after their custom, and then went out of the cave. 2 But they became sick from the food they had eaten because they were not used to it, so they went about in the cave saying to each other: 3 "What has our eating caused to happen to us, that we should be in such pain? We are in misery. We are going to die! It would have been better for us to have died keeping our bodies pure than to have eaten and defiled them with food." 4 Then Adam said to Eve, "This pain did not come to us in the garden, neither did we eat such bad food there. Eve, do you think that God will plague us through the food that is in us, or that our insides will come out, or that God intends to kill us with this pain before He has fulfilled His promise to us?" 5 Then Adam besought the Lord and said, "O Lord, let us not perish because of the food we have eaten. O Lord, don't punish us, but deal with us according to Your great mercy, and do not forsake us until the day of the promise You have made us." 6 Then God looked at them, and then equipped them to be able to eat (fitted them for eating) food at once, as it is to this day, so that they should not perish. 7 Then Adam and Eve came back into the cave sorrowful and crying because of the alteration of their bodies. And they both knew from that hour that they were altered beings and all hope of returning to the garden was now lost, and they could not enter it again. 8 For now their bodies had strange functions and all flesh that requires food and drink for its existence

cannot be in the garden. 9 Then Adam said to Eve, "See, our hope is now lost and so is our faith that we will enter the garden. We no longer belong to the inhabitants of the garden but from now on we are earthy and of the dust, and of the inhabitants of the earth. We shall not return to the garden until the day in which God has promised to save us and to bring us again into the garden, as He promised us." 10 Then they prayed to God that He would have mercy on them. After this, their minds were quieted, their hearts were broken, and their longing was cooled down, and they were like strangers on earth. That night Adam and Eve spent in the cave, where they slept heavily because of the food they had eaten.

Chapter LXVI

1 When the morning of the day after they had eaten food came, Adam and Eve prayed in the cave, and Adam said to Eve, "Look, we asked God for food, and He gave it. But now let us also ask Him to give us a drink of water." 2 Then they got up, and went to the bank of the stream of water, that was on the south border of the garden, which they had thrown themselves in before. And they stood on the bank, and prayed to God that He would command them to drink the water. 3 Then the Word of God came to Adam, and said to him, "O Adam, your body has become brutish, and requires water to drink. Take some and drink it, you and Eve, then give thanks and praise." 4 Adam and Eve then went down to the stream and drank from it, until their bodies felt refreshed. After they drank, they praised God

and then returned to their cave, as was their custom. This happened at the end of eighty-three days. 5 Then on the eighty-fourth day, they took the two figs and hung them in the cave together with the leaves of the figs. To them these were a sign and a blessing from God. And they placed them there so that if their descendants came there they would see the wonderful things God had done for them. 6 Then Adam and Eve stood outside the cave again and asked God to show them some food with which they could nourish their bodies. 7 Then the Word of God came and said to him, "Adam, go down west of the cave until you come to a land that has dark soil, and there you will find food." 8 And Adam obeyed the Word of God and took Eve, and went down to a land that had dark soil and found wheat growing ripe in the ear, and figs to eat; and Adam rejoiced over it. 9 Then the Word of God came again to Adam, and said to him, "Take some of this wheat and make yourselves some bread with it, to nourish your body." And God gave Adam's heart wisdom to work the corn until it became bread. 10 Adam accomplished it all until he grew very faint and weak. He then returned to the cave rejoicing at what he had learned what he had done with the wheat, until it was made into bread.

The word, "corn" is used to mean a seed. However, the sentence indicates it is a seed of wheat that is used to make bread. The words for corn, meaning a seed, and wheat, are used to mean the same thing. In Egypt there is a type of wheat called Durra. The seed (corn) of wheat was likely Durra.

Chapter LXVII

1 When Adam and Eve went down to the land of black earth (mud)
and came near to the wheat God had showed them and saw that it
was ripe and ready for reaping, they did not have a sickle to reap it
with. So they put themselves to the task and began to pull up the
wheat by hand until the task was complete. 2 They then heaped it
into a pile. They were weak from heat and from thirst and went
under a shady tree where the breeze fanned them to sleep. 3 But
Satan saw what Adam and Eve had done and he called his hosts, and
said to them, "God has shown to Adam and Eve all about this wheat
to strengthen their bodies, and, look, they have come and made a big
pile of it. Now they are weak from the toil are now asleep. Come, let
us set fire to this heap of corn (wheat seed), and burn it. Let us take
that bottle of water that is by them and empty it out, so that they may
find nothing to drink, and we kill them with hunger and thirst. 4
Then, when they wake up from their sleep and seek to return to the
cave, we will come to them along the way and lead them in the
wrong direction (get them lost) so that they die of hunger and thirst.
Then perhaps they will reject God, and He may destroy them. So, in
this way we can be rid of them." 5 Then Satan and his hosts set the
wheat on fire and burned it up. 6 But from the heat of the flame
Adam and Eve awoke from their sleep and saw the wheat burning
and the bucket of water by them was poured out. 7 Then they cried
and began to go back to the cave. 8 But as they were going up from

below the mountain, Satan and his hosts met them in the form of angels, praising God. 9 Then Satan said to Adam, "Adam, why are you so pained with hunger and thirst? It seems to me that Satan has burnt up the wheat." And Adam said to him, "Yes." 10 Satan said to Adam, "Come back with us. We are angels of God. God sent us to you to show you another field of corn (wheat) better than that, and beyond it is a fountain of good water and many trees, near where you shall live. And you shall work the corn field and make it better than that which Satan has consumed." 11 Adam thought that he was true, and that they were angels who talked with him and so he went back with them. 12 Then Satan began to lead Adam and Eve in the wrong direction for eight days, until they both fell down as if dead, from hunger, thirst, and weakness. Then he fled with his hosts, and left them.

Author's note: In this recurring theme of deceit by Satan, we are confronted by the age-old question in life; is the circumstance that confronts us an opportunity from God or a detour and trap of Satan. How are we to know?

Chapter LXVIII

1 Then God looked at Adam and Eve, and at what had befallen them from Satan, and how he killed them. 2 So, God sent His Word and raised Adam and Eve from of death. 3 Then, when he was raised, Adam said, "O God, You have burnt and taken the seeds which You had given us. You have emptied out the bucket of water. And You

have sent Your angels, who have caused us to lose our way from the corn (wheat) field. Will You kill us? If this is from you, O God, then take away our souls but stop punishing us." 4 Then God said to Adam, "I did not burn down the wheat, and I did not pour the water out of the bucket, and I did not send My angels to lead you astray. 5 But it is Satan, your master who did it. It was he to whom you have subjected yourself, while setting my commandment aside. It is He who burnt down the corn (wheat), and poured out the water, and who has led you astray. All the promises he has made you were just a trick, a deception, and a lie. 6 But now, Adam, you shall acknowledge My good deeds done to you." 7 And God told His angels to take Adam and Eve, and to lift them up to the field of wheat, which they found as before with the bucket full of water. 8 There they saw a tree and found on it solid manna, and they were astonished at God's power. And the angels commanded them to eat of the manna when they were hungry. 9 And God admonished Satan with a curse, not to come again and destroy the field of corn (wheat). 10 Then Adam and Eve took of the corn (wheat / seeds), and made an offering of it, and took it and offered it up on the mountain, at the place where they had offered up their first offering of blood. 11 And they offered this offering again on the altar they had built at first. And they stood up and prayed, and besought the Lord saying, "O God, when we were in the garden, our praises went up to you like this offering, and our innocence went up to you like incense. But now, O God, accept this offering from us, and don't turn us away or deprive us of Your mercy." 12 Then God said to Adam and Eve,

"Since you have made this offering and have offered it to Me, I shall make it My flesh when I come down on earth to save you. I shall cause it to be offered continually on an altar for forgiveness and mercy for those who partake of it appropriately." 13 Then God sent a bright fire over the offering of Adam and Eve and filled it with brightness, grace, and light. And the Holy Spirit came down on that offering. 14 Then God commanded an angel to take fire tongs, like a spoon, and take an offering and bring it to Adam and Eve. And the angel did so as God had commanded him, and offered it to them. 15 And the souls of Adam and Eve were brightened, and their hearts were filled with joy and gladness and with the praises of God. 16 And God said to Adam, "This shall be a custom to you to perform when affliction and sorrow should come over you. But your deliverance and your entrance in to the garden, shall not be until the days are fulfilled as agreed between you and Me. If it were not for this, I would bring you back to My garden and to My favor and My mercy and pity for you, for the sake of the offering you have just made to My name." 17 Adam rejoiced at these words, which he heard from God. And Adam and Eve worshipped before the altar, to which they bowed, and then went back to the Cave of Treasures. 18 And this took place at the end of the twelfth day after the eightieth day (92 days), from the time Adam and Eve came out of the garden. 19 And they stood up the entire night praying until morning. Then they went out of the cave. 20 Then Adam said to Eve, with joy in his heart, because of the offering they had made to God that had been accepted by Him, "Let us do this three times every week, on all the days of our life." 21 And as they agreed on these words and God was pleased with their thoughts and with the decision they made. 22 After this, the Word of God came to Adam, and said, "Adam, you have determined beforehand the days in which sufferings shall come over Me, when I am made flesh. They are the fourth day, which is Wednesday, and the preparation day, which is Friday. 23 But regarding the first day, I created all things in it, and I raised the heavens. Through My rising again on this day, will I create joy and raise them who believe in Me on high. Adam, make this offering all the days of your life." 24 Then the Word of God withdrew from Adam. 25 But Adam continued to make the offering as he had, every week, three times a week, until the end of seven weeks. And on the first day, which is the fiftieth, Adam made an offering as he was accustomed, and he and Eve took it and came to the altar before God, as He had taught them.

Author's note: The order and number of the days of the week are called out as follows, "the fourth day, Wednesday, on the preparation day Friday, and on the Sabbath Sunday." The Jewish Sabbath is from Friday at sundown to Saturday at sundown, wherein, Saturday is considered to be the Sabbath. The shift shows Christian influence and a dating later than the writer(s) would have us believe.

Chapter LXIX

1 Then Satan, the hater of all that is good, was envious of Adam the

fact that his offering found favor with God. So Satan hurried and took a sharp stone from among the sharp ironstones, which were shaped in the form of a man. And Satan went and stood by Adam and Eve. 2 Adam was offering on the altar and had begun to pray with his hands spread before God. 3 Then Satan hurried with the sharp ironstone he had and pierced Adam on the right side, and blood and water flowed. Then Adam fell on the altar like a corpse, and Satan fled. 4 Then Eve came and took Adam and placed him below the altar. There she stayed, crying over him while a stream of blood flowed from Adam's side over his offering. 5 But God looked at the death of Adam. He then sent His Word and raised him up. And He said to him, "Fulfill your offering because, certainly Adam, it is worthy and there is no imperfection in it." 6 God continued speaking to Adam, "Thus will it also happen to Me while on the earth, when I shall be pierced and blood and water shall flow from My side and run over My body, which is the true offering, and which shall be offered on the altar as a perfect offering." 7 Then God commanded Adam to finish his offering. And when he had ended it he worshipped before God and praised Him for the signs He had showed him. 8 And God healed Adam in one day, which is the end of the seven weeks and is the fiftieth day. 9 Then Adam and Eve returned from the mountain and went into the Cave of Treasures, as they were used to do. This completed one hundred and forty days for Adam and Eve, since their coming out of the garden. 10 Then they both stood up that night and prayed to God. And when it was morning they went down to the west side of the cave, to the place where their wheat (corn) was, and there they rested under the shadow of a tree, as they were accustomed to do. 11 But when they were there, a multitude of beasts came all around them. It was Satan's wickedness and his way to wage war against Adam through marriage.

Author's note: The following chapter will explain how marriage fits into Satan's plan. The fact that Satan will use marriage against Adam and Eve indicates that the writer of this text viewed marriage in a less than positive light. It should also be stressed that the idea of a ceremony is not the point of marriage in this context. It is intercourse that establishes the state. The resulting children and complications were the point of Satan's plan.

Chapter LXX

1 After this Satan, the hater of all that is good, took the form of an angel, and two others with him. So, they looked like the three angels who had brought to Adam gold, incense, and myrrh. 2 They came to Adam and Eve while they were under the tree, and greeted Adam and Eve with friendly words that were full of deceit. 3 But when Adam and Eve saw their friendly countenance and heard their sweet speech, Adam rose, welcomed them, and brought them to Eve and they remained all together. Adam's heart was happy all the while because he thought that they were the same angels, who had brought him gold, incense, and myrrh. 4 This was because when they came to Adam the first time peace and joy came over him from them because

they brought him good gifts. So Adam thought that they had come a second time to give him other gifts to make him rejoice. He did not know it was Satan, therefore he received them with joy and associated with them. 5 Then Satan, the tallest of them, said, "Rejoice, Adam, and be glad. Look, God has sent us to you to tell you something." 6 And Adam said, "What is it?" Then Satan said, "It is a simple thing, but it is the Word of God. Will you accept it from us and do it? If you will not accept it, we will return to God and tell Him that you would not receive His Word." 7 And Satan continued, saying to Adam, "Don't be afraid and don't shake. Don't you know us?" 8 But Adam said, "I do not know you." 9 Then Satan said to him, "I am the angel that brought you gold and took it to the cave. This other angel is the one that brought you incense. And that third angel is the one who brought you myrrh when you were on top of the mountain. It was he who carried you to the cave. 10 It was our other fellow angels who lifted you to the cave. God has not sent them with us this time because He said to us, 'You will be enough'. " 11 So when Adam heard these words he believed them, and said to the angels, "Speak the Word of God, and I will receive it." 12 And Satan said to him, "Swear and promise me that you will receive it." 13 Then Adam said, "I do not know how to swear and promise." 14 And Satan said to him, "Hold out your hand and put it inside my hand." 15 Then Adam held out his hand, and put it into Satan's hand. Satan said to him, "Now say this; As God who raised the stars in heaven, and established the dry ground on the waters, and has created me out of the four elements, and out of the dust of the earth, and is logical and true does speak, I will not break my promise, nor abandon my word." 16 And Adam swore. 17 Then Satan said to him, "Look, some time has passed since you came out of the garden, and you do not know wickedness or evil. But now God says to you, to take Eve who came out of your side, and marry her so that she will bear you children to comfort you and to drive from you trouble and sorrow. This thing is not difficult and there is nothing morally wrong in it for you.

Chapter LXXI

1 But when Adam heard these words from Satan, he sorrowed much, because of his oath and his promise. And he said, "Shall I commit adultery with my flesh and my bones, and shall I sin against myself, so that God will destroy me blot me out from the face of the earth? 2 First, I ate of the tree and He drove me out of the garden into this strange land and deprived me of my bright nature, and brought my death. If I do this, He will cut off my life from the earth, and He will cast me into hell, and plague me there a long time. 3 But God never spoke the words that you have said and you are not God's angels. He did not send you. You are devils that have come to me under the false appearance of angels. Away from me, you cursed of God!" 4 Then the devils fled from Adam. And he and Eve got up and returned to the Cave of Treasures, and went into it. 5 Then Adam said to Eve, "If you saw what I did, don't tell anyone because I sinned against God in swearing by His great name, and I have placed my

hand once again into that of Satan." Eve then held her peace as Adam told her. 6 Then Adam got up and spread his hands before God, beseeching and entreating Him with tears to forgive him of what he had done. And Adam remained standing and praying in that way for forty days and forty nights. He did not eat or drink until he dropped down on the ground from hunger and thirst. 7 Then God sent His Word to Adam, who raised him up from where he lay, and said to him, "Adam, why have you sworn by My name? Why have you made agreement with Satan again?" 8 But Adam cried and said, "O God, forgive me. I did this unwittingly because I believed they were God's angels." 9 And God forgave Adam and said to him, "Beware of Satan." 10 And He withdrew His Word from Adam. 11 Then Adam's heart was comforted, and he took Eve and they went out of the cave to prepare some food for their bodies. 12 But from that day Adam struggled in his mind about marrying Eve, because he was afraid that if he did it, God would be angry with him. 13 Then Adam and Eve went to the river of water, and sat on the bank, as people do when they enjoy themselves. 14 But Satan was jealous of them and planned to destroy them.

Author's note: Clearly, Adam viewed copulating with Eve as incest and therefore morally wrong, even though it was not yet law. The idea kindled his desire, which was in opposition to what Adam viewed as a moral issue. This issue will be visited again in other texts such as Jubliees and others as Cain's marriage to his sister is addressed.

Chapter LXXII

1 Then Satan, and ten from his hosts, transformed themselves into maidens, with more grace than any others in the entire world. 2 They came up out of the river in front of Adam and Eve, and they said among themselves, "Come, we will look at the faces of Adam and Eve who are of the men on earth. They are beautiful and their faces look different than ours." Then they came to Adam and Eve and greeted them, and they stood amazed at them. 3 Adam and Eve looked at them also, and wondered at their beauty, and said, "Is there another world under us with such beautiful creatures as these in it?" 4 And the maidens said to Adam and Eve, "Yes, indeed, many of us were created." 5 Then Adam said to them, "But how do you multiply?" 6 And they told him, "We have husbands who have married us and we bear them children, who grow up and in turn marry and are married and also bear children. Thus we increase. O Adam, you will not believe us, we will show you our husbands and our children." 7 Then they shouted over the river as if to call their husbands and their children. And men and children came up from the river, and every man came to his wife, and his children were with him. 8 But when Adam and Eve saw them, they stood speechless and were amazed at them. 9 Then they said to Adam and Eve, "See all our husbands and our children? You should marry Eve as we have married our husbands so that you will have children as we have."

This was the way Satan was to deceive Adam. 10 Satan also thought to himself, "God at first commanded Adam concerning the fruit of the tree, saying to him, 'Do not eat of it or else you shall die.' But Adam ate of it but God did not kill him. He only gave him by law death, plagues, and trials, until the day he shall leave his body. 11 But if I deceive him to do this thing and marry Eve without God's permission, God will kill him." 12 Therefore Satan worked this apparition before Adam and Eve, because he sought to kill him, and to make him disappear from off the face of the earth. 13 Meanwhile the fire of immorality came over Adam and he thought of committing transgression. But he restrained himself, fearing that if he followed the advice of Satan, God would put him to death. 14 Then Adam and Eve got up and prayed to God, while Satan and his hosts went down into the river in front of Adam and Eve so they would see them going back to their own world. 15 Then Adam and Eve went back to the Cave of Treasures, as they usually did around evening time. 16 And they both got up and prayed to God that night. Adam remained standing in prayer but did not know how to pray because of the thoughts in his heart about marrying Eve. And he continued this way until morning. 17 When light came up, Adam said to Eve, "Get up, let us go below the mountain where they brought us gold and let us ask the Lord concerning this matter." 18 Then Eve said, "What is that matter, Adam?" 19 And he answered her, "That I may request the Lord to inform me about marrying you because I will not do it without His permission or else He will kill you and me. For those devils have set my heart on fire with thoughts of what they showed us in their sinful visions. 20 Then Eve said to Adam, "Why do we need to go to the foot of the mountain? Let us rather stand up and pray in our cave to God to let us know whether this advice is good or not." 21 Then Adam rose up in prayer and said, "O God, you know that we transgressed against you, and from the moment we sinned we were stripped of our bright nature, and our body became brutish, requiring food and drink, and with animal desires. 22 Command us, O God, not to give way to them without Your permission, for fear that You will turn us into nothing. If you do not give us permission we will be overcome and follow that advice of Satan, and You will again kill us. 23 If not, then take our souls from us and let us be rid of this animal lust. And if You give us no order about this thing then separate Eve from me and me from her, and place us each far away from the other. 24 Then, O God, if You separate us from each other the devils will deceive us with their apparitions that resemble us, and destroy our hearts, and defile our thoughts towards each other. If our heart is not toward each other it will be toward them, through their appearance when the devils come to us in our likeness." Here Adam ended his prayer.

Chapter LXXIII

1 Then God considered the words of Adam that they were true, and that he could not wait long for His order, respecting the counsel of Satan. 2 And God approved Adam in what he had thought concerning this, and in the prayer he had offered in His presence;

and the Word of God came to Adam and said to him, "O Adam, if only you had had this caution at first, before you came out of the garden into this land!" 3 After that, God sent His angel who had brought gold, and the angel who had brought incense, and the angel who had brought myrrh to Adam, that they should inform him respecting his marriage to Eve. 4 Then those angels said to Adam, "Take the gold and give it to Eve as a wedding gift, and promise to marry her; then give her some incense and myrrh as a present; and be you both will be one flesh." 5 Adam obeyed the angels, and took the gold and put it into Eve's bosom in her garment; and promised to marry her with his hand. 6 Then the angels commanded Adam and Eve to get up and pray forty days and forty nights; when that was done, then Adam was to have sexual intercourse with his wife; for then this would be an act pure and undefiled; so that he would have children who would multiply, and replenish the face of the earth. 7 Then both Adam and Eve received the words of the angels; and the angels departed from them. 8 Then Adam and Eve began to fast and pray, until the end of the forty days; and then they had sexual intercourse, as the angels had told them. And from the time Adam left the garden until he wedded Eve, were two hundred and twenty-three days, that is seven months and thirteen days. 9 This was how Satan's war with Adam was won by Adam and Satan was defeated.

Author's note: In the apocryphal book of Tobit, the main character goes into his new bride after praying to still his lust and was thus pure.

The word "replenish" indicates that the earth was once full or "plenished" and was to be "replenished" or filled again. This is the same word used in Genesis, leading two the Second Creation Theory.

Chapter LXXIV

1 And they lived on the earth working so they could keep their bodies in good health. And they continued until the nine months of Eve's pregnancy were over and the time drew near when she would give birth. 2 Then she said to Adam, "The tokens placed in this cave since we left the garden show it to be a pure place. We will be praying in it again in a while. Because of this, it is not appropriate that I should give birth in it. Let us instead go to the sheltering rock cave that was formed by the command of God when Satan threw a big rock down on us in an attempt to kill us. 3 Adam then took Eve to that cave. When the time came for her to give birth she strained very much. Adam felt pity for her and he was very worried about her because she was close to death and the words of God to her were being fulfilled: " You shall bear a child in suffering, and in sorrow shall you bring forth a child." 4 But when Adam saw the distress Eve was in, he got up and prayed to God, and said, "O Lord, look at me with the eye of Your mercy, and deliver her out of her distress." 5 And God looked at His maid-servant Eve, and delivered her, and she gave birth to her first-born son, and with him a daughter. 6 Then Adam rejoiced at Eve's deliverance, and also over the children she had given him. And Adam ministered to Eve in the cave until the end of eight days, when they named the son Cain, and the daughter

Luluwa. 7 The meaning of Cain is "hater," because he hated his sister in their mother's womb, before they were born. Because of this, Adam named him Cain. 8 But Luluwa means "beautiful," because she was more beautiful than her mother. 9 Then Adam and Eve waited until Cain and his sister were forty days old, when Adam said to Eve, "We will make an offering and offer it up in behalf of the children." 10 And Eve said, "We will first make one offering for the first-born son and then later we shall make one for the daughter."

Author's note: Jewish law says the woman is unclean for a time after giving birth. The act, having human blood present, makes the place unclean. The first cave served as home and temple. The second cave served as a place of safety and shelter.

It will be noted the each time Eve gave birth she did so with twins, symbolizing the replenishing or replacing of Adam and Eve.

Chapter LXXV

1 Then Adam prepared an offering. He and Eve brought it to the altar they had built at first and offered it up for their children. 2 And Adam offered up the offering, and asked God to accept his offering. 3 Then God accepted Adam's offering, and sent a light from heaven that shined down on the offering. Adam and his son drew near to the offering, but Eve and the daughter did not approach it. 4 Adam and his son were joyful as they came down from the altar. Adam and Eve waited until the daughter was eighty days old and then Adam

prepared an offering and took it to Eve and to the children. They went to the altar where Adam offered it up, as he was accustomed, asking the Lord to accept his offering. 5 And the Lord accepted the offering of Adam and Eve. Then Adam, Eve, and the children gathered together and came down from the mountain, rejoicing. 6 But they did not return to the cave in which they were born. Instead they went to the Cave of Treasures, so that the children should live in it and be blessed with the tokens brought from the garden. 7 But after they had been blessed with the tokens they went back to the cave in which they were born. 8 But, before Eve had offered up the offering, Adam had taken her to the river of water in which they threw themselves at first. There they washed themselves. Adam washed his body and Eve washed hers clean also, after the suffering and distress that had come over them. 9 But after washing themselves in the river of water, Adam and Eve returned every night to the Cave of Treasures, where they prayed and were blessed, and then went back to their cave where their children were born. 10 Adam and Eve did this until the children had been weaned. After they were weaned, Adam made an offering for the souls of his children in addition to the three times every week he made an offering for them. 11 When the children were weaned, Eve conceived again, and when her pregnancy came to term, she gave birth to another son and daughter. They named the son Abel and the daughter Aklia. 12 Then at the end of forty days, Adam made an offering for the son, and at the end of eighty days he made another offering for the daughter, and treated them as he had previously treated Cain and his sister Luluwa. 13 He brought them to the Cave of Treasures, where they received a blessing and then returned to the cave where they were born. After these children were born, Eve stopped having children.

Author's note: To compare the purification ritual recounted here to those of the Old Testament we look to the book of the law. Leviticus 12 (RSV) 1 The LORD said to Moses, 2"Say to the people of Israel, If a woman conceives, and bears a male child, then she shall be unclean seven days; as at the time of her menstruation, she shall be unclean. 3 And on the eighth day the flesh of his foreskin shall be circumcised. 4 Then she shall continue for thirty-three days in the blood of her purifying; she shall not touch any hallowed thing, nor come into the sanctuary, until the days of her purifying are completed. 5 But if she bears a female child, then she shall be unclean two weeks, as in her menstruation; and she shall continue in the blood of her purifying for sixty-six days. 6 "And when the days of her purifying are completed, whether for a son or for a daughter, she shall bring to the priest at the door of the tent of meeting a lamb a year old for a burnt offering, and a young pigeon or a turtledove for a sin offering , 7 and he shall offer it before the LORD, and make atonement for her; then she shall be clean from the flow of her blood. This is the law for her who bears a child, either male or female. 8 And if she cannot afford a lamb, then she shall take two turtledoves or two young pigeons, one for a burnt offering and the other for a sin offering; and the priest shall make atonement for her, and she shall be clean."

Chapter LXXVI

1 As the children began to grow stronger and taller, Cain grew hard-
hearted, and he ruled over his younger brother. 2 Often, when his
father made an offering, Cain would remain behind and not go with
them to make the offering. 3 But Abel had a meek heart, and was
obedient to his father and mother. He frequently influenced them to
make an offering because he loved it. He prayed and fasted much. 4
Then this sign came to Abel. As he was coming into the Cave of
Treasures he saw the golden rods, the incense and the myrrh and he
asked his parents, Adam and Eve, to tell him about them. Abel
asked, "Where did you get these from?" 5 Then Adam told him all
that had befallen them. And Abel felt deeply about what his father
told him. 6 Then his father, Adam, told him about the works of God
and of the garden. After hearing these things, Abel remained behind
after his father left and stayed the entire of that night in the Cave of
Treasures. 7 And that night, while he was praying, Satan appeared to
him in the form of a man. And Satan said to him, "Often you have
moved your father into making offerings, and to fast and pray.
Because of this, I will kill you and make you perish from this world."
8 But Abel prayed to God and drove away Satan, and he did not
believe the words of the devil. Then when it was day, an angel of
God appeared to him, who said to him, "Do not stop your fasting,
prayer, or offering to your God. For, look, the Lord has accepted your
prayer. Be not afraid of the form which appeared to you in the night,
and who cursed you to death." Then the angel departed from him. 9

Then Abel came to Adam and Eve when it was day, and told them about the vision he had seen. When they heard it they worried about it very much, but said nothing to him about it. They only comforted him. 10 But Satan came to the hard-hearted Cain by night and showed himself and said to him, "Since Adam and Eve love your brother Abel so much more than they love you, they wish to join him in marriage to your beautiful sister because they love him. However, they wish to join you in marriage to his ugly sister, because they hate you. 11 Now before they do that, I am telling you that you should kill your brother. That way your sister will be left for you and you can throw his sister away." 12 And Satan departed from him. But the devil remained behind in Cain's heart, and frequently prompted his ambition to kill his brother.

Author's note: Since the children were born in pairs, it seems more reasonable to have those that were not twins marry.

Note the word used in reference to Cain's heart. He was hard-hearted and the devil gave him ambition – or hope – or aspiration to kill. As if this were something to achieve as a noble end.

Chapter LXXVII

1 But when Adam saw that the older brother hated the younger brother, he attempted to soften their hearts. He said to Cain, "My son, take some of the fruits of your sowing and make an offering to God, so that He might forgive you for your wickedness and your sin." 2

He said also to Abel, "Take some of the fruit of your sowing and make an offering and bring it to God, so that He might forgive you for your wickedness and your sin." 3 Then Abel obeyed his father and took some of his sowing, and made a good offering, and said to his father, Adam, "Come with me and show me how to offer it up." 4 And they went, Adam and Eve with him, and they showed him how to offer up his gift on the altar. Then after that they stood up and prayed that God would accept Abel's offering. 5 Then God looked at Abel and accepted his offering. And God was more pleased with Abel than He was with his offering, because of his good heart and pure body. There was no trace of guile in him. 6 Then they came down from the altar and went to the cave in which they lived. But because of his joy felt at making his offering, Abel repeated it three times a week, following the example of his father Adam. 7 But Cain did not want to make an offering, but after his father became very angry, he offered up a gift once. He took the smallest of his sheep for an offering and when he offered it up, his eyes were on the lamb. 8 Because of this, God did not accept his offering, because his heart was full of murderous thoughts. 9 And they all lived together like this in the cave in which Eve had given birth, until Cain was fifteen years old, and Abel twelve years old.

Chapter LXXVIII

1 Then Adam said to Eve, "The children have grown up. We must think of finding wives for them." 2 Then Eve answered, "How can we

do that?" 3 Then Adam said to her, "We will join Abel's sister in
marriage to Cain, and Cain's sister to Abel. 4 Then Eve said to Adam,
"I do not like Cain because he is hard-hearted. So, let them stay with
us until we offer up (an offering) to the Lord in their behalf." 5 And
Adam said no more. 6 Meanwhile Satan came to Cain in the form of a
man of the field, and said to him, "Look. Adam and Eve have
discussed together about the marriage of you two, and they have
agreed to marry Abel's sister to you, and your sister to Abel. 7 But if
it were not that I love you, I would not have told you this thing. So, if
you will take my advice and obey me, I will bring beautiful robes,
plenty of gold and silver, and my relations will attend you on your
wedding day." 8 Then Cain said with joy, "Where are your relations?"
9 And Satan answered, "My relations are in a garden in the north,
where I once meant to bring your father Adam, but he would not
accept my offer. 10 But if you will receive my words and if you will
come to me after your wedding, you shall rest from the misery in
which you are; and you shall rest and be better off than your father
Adam." 11 At these words, Satan got Cain's attention (opened his
ears), and Cain inclined toward Satan to listen (leaned towards his
speech). 12 After this, he did not remain in the field, but he went to
Eve, his mother, and beat her and cursed her, and said to her, "Why
are you planning to take my sister to marry her to my brother? Am I
dead?" 13 But his mother quieted him and sent him back to the field
where he had been. 14 Then when Adam came, she told him of what
Cain had done. 15 Adam was very worried, but held his peace, and
did not say a word. 16 Then, the next morning Adam said to Cain his

son, "Take of your young and good sheep and offer them up to your God, and I will speak to your brother and have him make an offering of corn to his God." 17 They both obeyed their father Adam, and they took their offerings, and offered them up on the mountain by the altar. 18 But Cain behaved arrogantly (haughtily) toward his brother, and he shoved him from the altar, and would not let him offer up his gift on the altar, but he offered his own offering on it with a proud heart, full of guile and fraud. 19 But Abel set up stones that were near at hand and on that, he offered up his gift with a heart humble and free from guile. 20 Cain was then standing by the altar on which he had offered up his gift and he cried to God to accept his offering, but God did not accept it from Cain, nor did a divine fire come down to consume his offering. 21 But he remained standing over against the altar out of meanness, to make fun of his brother, and he glared at his brother Abel to see if God would accept his offering or not. 22 And Abel prayed to God to accept his offering. Then a divine fire came down and consumed his offering. And God smelled the sweet savor of his offering, because Abel loved Him and rejoice in Him. 23 And because God was well pleased with him, He sent him an angel of light in the form of a man to partake of his offering, because He had smelled the sweet savor of his offering, and he comforted Abel and strengthened his heart. 24 But Cain was looking on all that took place at his brother's offering, and was angry because of it. 25 Then he opened his mouth and blasphemed God because He had not accepted his offering. 26 But God said to Cain, "Why do you look sad? Be in right standing with Me so that I may accept your offering.

You have not murmured against Me, but against yourself. 27 And
God said this to Cain in rebuke, and because He hated him and his
offering. 28 And Cain came down from the altar and his color
changed and he had a sad face. And he came to his father and
mother and told them all that had happened to him. And Adam
grieved much because God had not accepted Cain's offering. 29 But
Abel came down rejoicing, and with a glad heart, and told his father
and mother how God had accepted his offering. And they rejoiced at
it and kissed his face. 30 And Abel said to his father, "Because Cain
shoved me from the altar, and would not allow me to offer my gift on
it, I made an altar for myself and offered my gift on it."
31 But when Adam heard this he was very sorry because it was the
altar he had built at first, and on which he had offered his own gifts.
32 Cain was so resentful and so angry that he went into the field.
There, Satan came to him and said to him, "Your brother Abel has
taken refuge with your father Adam, because you shoved him from
the altar. They have kissed his face and they rejoice over him far
more than over you." 33 When Cain heard these words of Satan he
was filled with rage but he let no one know. But he was laying in
wait to kill his brother, until he brought him into the cave, and then
said to him: 34 "Brother, the country is so beautiful and there are
such beautiful and pleasurable trees in it, and charming to look at!
But brother, you have never been one day in the field to take your
pleasure in that place. 35 Today, my brother, I wish very much that
you would come into the field with me, to enjoy yourself and to bless
our fields and our flocks, for you are righteous, and I love you much,

O my brother! But you have alienated yourself from me." 36 Then Abel agreed to go with his brother Cain into the field. 37 But before going out, Cain said to Abel, "Wait for me and I will fetch a staff because of wild beasts." 38 Then Abel stood innocently waiting. But Cain, the presumptuous, got a staff and went out. 39 And Cain and his brother Abel began to walk in the path. Cain was talking to him, and comforting him, to make him forget everything.

Chapter LXXIX

1 And so they walked on until they came to a place they were alone where there were no sheep. Then Abel said to Cain, "Look, my brother, we are tired from walking. We see none of the trees, or fruits, or the growing green plants, or the sheep, or any of the things of which you told me. Where are those sheep of yours that you told me to bless?" 2 Then Cain said to him, "Come on, and you shall see many beautiful things very soon, but go before me until I catch up to you." 3 Then Abel went on but Cain stayed behind him. 4 And Abel was innocently walking, without suspecting any craftiness, not thinking that his brother would kill him. 5 Then Cain came up to him, comforted him with his words while walking a little behind him. Then he ran up to him and beat him with the staff, blow after blow, until he was dazed. 6 But when Abel fell down on the ground and saw that his brother meant to kill him, he said to Cain, "O, my brother, have pity on me. By the breasts we have sucked, do not hit me! By the womb that bore us and that brought us into the world, do

not beat me to death with that staff! If you are set on killing me, take one of these large stones and kill me outright." 7 Then Cain, the hard-hearted, and cruel murderer, took a large stone, and beat his brother's head with it until his brains oozed out, and he wallowed in his blood, before him. 8 And Cain was not sorry for what he had done. 9 But when the blood of righteous Abel fell on the earth, it trembled as it drank his blood, and would have destroyed Cain because of it. 10 And the blood of Abel cried mysteriously to God to avenge him of his murderer. 11 Then Cain began to dig furiously at the ground to bury his brother, because he was shaking from fear that came over him when he saw the earth tremble because of him. 12 He then threw his brother into the hole he made, and covered him with dust. But the ground would not receive him and it threw him up at once. 13 Again Cain dug the ground and covered his brother in it, but again the ground threw him up. Three times the ground threw up the body of Abel on itself. 14 The muddy ground threw him up the first time because he was not the first creation. It threw him up the second time and would not receive him because he was righteous and good and was killed without a cause. The ground threw him up the third time and would not receive him so that there might remain before his brother a witness against him. 15 And so the earth mocked Cain until the Word of God came to him concerning his brother. 16 Then God was angry and very much displeased at Abel's death. And He thundered from heaven, and lightning went out from Him, and the Word of the Lord God came from heaven to Cain, and said to him, "Where is Abel, your brother?" 17 Then Cain answered with a proud heart and a gruff voice, "How am I to know, O God? Am I my brother's keeper?" 18 Then God said to Cain, "Cursed be the earth that has drunk the blood of Abel, your brother. And as for you, you will always be trembling and shaking, and this will be a mark on you so that whoever finds you will kill you." 19 But Cain cried because God had said those words to him. And Cain said to Him, "O God, whosoever finds me shall kill me, and I shall be blotted out from the face of the earth." 20 Then God said to Cain, "Whoever finds you will not kill you," because before this, God had been saying to Cain, "I shall put seven punishments on anyone that kills Cain." For the word of God to Cain was, "Where is your brother?" God said it in mercy to him, to try and make him repent. 21 And if Cain had repented at that time, and had said, "O God, forgive me my sin, and the murder of my brother," God would then have forgiven him his sin. 22 But God said to Cain, "Cursed be the ground that has drunk the blood of your brother" That also, was God's mercy on Cain, because God did not curse him, but He cursed the ground, although it was not the ground that had killed Abel, and committed a wicked sin. 23 But it was fitting that the curse should fall on the murderer, and yet, in mercy did God managed His thoughts so that no one should know the extent of His anger for He turned it away from Cain. 24 And He said to him, "Where is your brother?" To which he answered and said, "I know not." Then the Creator said to him, "Be trembling and quaking." 25 Then Cain trembled and became terrified, and through this sign God made him an example before all the creation to show him as the murderer of his brother. Also God brought trembling and terror over him so that he might see the peace he had before and also see the trembling and terror he endured at the end, so that he might humble himself before God and repent of his sin, and seek the peace that he enjoyed at first. 26 The word of God said, "I will put seven punishments on anyone who kills Cain." So, God was not seeking to kill Cain with the sword, but He sought to make him die of fasting, and praying, and crying by His discipline, until the time that he was delivered from his sin. 27 And the seven punishments are the seven generations during which God awaited Cain for the murder of his brother. 28 But, ever since he had killed his brother, Cain could find no rest in any place, so he went back to Adam and Eve, trembling, terrified, and defiled with blood.

This ends The First Book of Adam and Eve

Author's note: Wallowing in the blood of a kill coveys an extreme in animal behavior and state.

What is amazing about this chapter is the limits explored to explain the thoughts, actions, and strategy of God toward Cain. We are told that the enigmatic mark left on Cain as a curse is actually the physical trait of shaking and trembling in fear. One may ask if this is the mark of cowardice exhibited by a bully.

The explanation of God's first statement to kill Cain, then cursing anyone who would kill Cain, then "waiting for Cain seven generations is wordy, convoluted, and odd. The author seems to be attempting to put all of the pieces together in some reasonable manner. This could be due to the knitting together of several sources with the last man left with the task of tying the story together into a cohesive conclusion.

Joseph B. Lumpkin

The Second Book of Adam and Eve

The Second Book of Adam and Eve expands on the time from Cain's act of murder to the time Enoch was taken by God. It is, above all, a continuation of the story of *The First Book of Adam and Eve*.

Like the first book, this book is also part of the "Pseudepigrapha", which is a collection of historical biblical works that are considered to be fiction. Although considered to be Pseudepigrapha, it carries significance in that it provides insight into what was considered acceptable religious writing and ideas of the time.

This book is a composite of oral versions of an account handed down by word of mouth, from generation to generation until an unknown author pieced the stories together into a written form.

This particular version is the work of unknown Egyptians. The lack of historical allusion makes it difficult to date the writing. Using other Pseudepigrapha works as a reference only slightly narrows the probable dates to a range of a few hundred years. Parts of the text were probably included in an oral tradition, two or three hundred years before the birth of Christ. Certainly, book two was written after book one.

Sections of the text are found in the Jewish Talmud, and the Islamic Koran. Although some think this shows how the books of

Adam and Eve played a vital role in ancient literature, it could just as well expose the fact that the authors of the Adam and Eve stories borrowed heavily from accepted holy books.

The Egyptian author wrote in Arabic, but later translations were found written in Ethiopic. The present English translation was completed in the late 1800's by Dr. S. C. Malan and Dr. E. Trumpp. They translated the text into King James English from both the Arabic version and the Ethiopic version, which was then published in The Forgotten Books of Eden in 1927 by The World Publishing Company. The version presented here takes the 1927 version, written in King James style English, and renders it into wording more familiar to the modern reader. Tangled sentence structure and archaic words were replaced with a more clear, crisp, twenty-first century English.

Second Book of Adam and Eve

Chapter I.

1 When Luluwa heard Cain's words, she wept and went to call her father and mother, and told them how Cain had killed his brother Abel.

2 Then they all cried aloud and lifted up their voices, and slapped their faces, and threw dust upon their heads, and ripped their garments apart, and went out and came to the place where Abel was killed.

3 And they found him lying on the earth, killed, and beasts were around him. They wept and cried because he was a just person. Because his body was pure, from it went forth a smell of sweet spices.

4 And Adam carried him as Adam's tears streaming down his face; and he went to the Cave of Treasures, where he laid Abel, and Adam wound him up with sweet spices and myrrh.

5 And Adam and Eve continued in great grief by the burial site for a hundred and forty days. Abel was fifteen and a half years old, and Cain seventeen years and a half.

6 When the mourning for his brother was ended, Cain took his sister Luluwa and married her, without permission from his father and

mother. Because of their heavy hearts they could not keep him from her.

7 He then went down to the foot of the mountain, away from the garden, near the place where he had killed his brother.

8 And in that place were many fruit trees and forest trees. His sister gave birth to his children, who in their turn began to multiply by degrees until they filled that place.

9 But Adam and Eve did not come together (have intercourse) for seven years after Abel's funeral. After this, however, Eve conceived. And while she was with child Adam said to her, "Come, let us take an offering and offer it up unto God and ask Him to give us a beautiful child in whom we may find comfort, and whom we may join in marriage to Abel's sister."

10 Then they prepared an offering and brought it up to the altar, and offered it before the Lord, and began to ask Him to accept their offering and to give them a good offspring.

11 And God heard Adam and accepted his offering. Then, Adam, Eve and their daughter worshipped, and came down to the Cave of Treasures and placed a lamp in it by the body of Abel to burn by the body, night and day.

12 Then Adam and Eve continued fasting and praying until Eve's time came that she should be delivered, when she said to Adam, "I wish to go to the cave in the rock, to give birth in it."

13 And he said, "Go, and take your daughter with you to wait on you; but I will remain in this Cave of Treasures before the body of my son Abel."

14 Then Eve listened to Adam, and she and her daughter left, but Adam remained by himself in the Cave of Treasures.

Chapter II.

1 And Eve gave birth to a son, perfectly beautiful in form and in demeanor. His beauty was like that of his father Adam, yet more beautiful.

2 Then Eve was comforted when she saw him, and remained eight days in the cave; then she sent her daughter unto Adam to tell him to come and see the child and name him. But the daughter stayed in his place by the body of her brother, until Adam returned.

3 But when Adam came and saw the child's good looks, his beauty, and his perfect form, he rejoiced over him, and was comforted for Abel. Then he named the child Seth, which means, "that God has heard my prayer, and has delivered me out of my affliction." But it means also "power and strength."

4 Then after Adam had named the child, he returned to the Cave of Treasures; and his daughter went back to her mother.

5 But Eve continued in her cave, until forty days were fulfilled, when she came to Adam, and brought with her the child and her daughter.

6 And they came to a river of water, where Adam and his daughter washed themselves, because of their sorrow for Abel; but Eve and the babe washed for purification.

7 Then they returned, and took an offering, and went to the mountain and offered it up for the babe; and God accepted their

offering, and sent His blessing upon them, and upon their son Seth; and they came back to the Cave of Treasures.

8 As for Adam, he did not have intercourse again with his wife Eve, all the days of his life; neither was any more offspring born of them; but only those five, Cain, Luluwa, Abel, Aklia, and Seth alone.

9 But Seth waxed in stature and in strength; and began to fast and pray, fervently.

Author's note: Abel was fifteen and a half years old, and Cain seventeen years and a half when Abel was killed. Cain and Luluwa were twins. Abel and Aklia were twins. Cain married his twin sister. Aklia was fifteen and a half when Abel died. Adam and Eve did not come together (have intercourse) for seven years after Abel's funeral. Aklia would now be twenty-two and a half. Eve carried Seth for nine months. At the time of Seth's birth, Aklia would have been twenty-three years old.

Chapter III.

1 At the end of seven years from the day Adam had been separated from his wife Eve, Satan envied him, and when he saw Adam was separated from her, Satan strove to make him live with her again.

2 Then Adam arose and went up above the Cave of Treasures and continued to sleep there night by night. But every day as soon as it was light he came down to the cave to pray there and to receive a blessing from it.

3 But when it was evening he went up on the top of the cave, where

he slept by himself, fearing that Satan could overcome him. And he continued apart in this way for thirty-nine days.

4 Then when Satan, the hater of all that is good, saw Adam alone, fasting and praying, he appeared unto him in the form of a beautiful woman who came and stood in front of him in the night of the fortieth day, and said to him:

5 "Adam, from the time you have dwelt in this cave, we have experienced great peace from you, and your prayers have reached us, and we have been comforted because of you.

6 "But now, Adam, that you have gone up over the roof of the cave to sleep, we have had doubts about you, and a great sorrow has come upon us because of your separation from Eve. Then again, when you are on the roof of this cave, your prayer is poured out, and your heart wanders from side to side.

7 "But when you were in the cave your prayer was like fire gathered together. It came down to us, and you found rest.

8 "Then I also worried over your children who are separated from you, and my sorrow is great about the murder of your son Abel because he was righteous, and over a righteous man every one will grieve.

9 "But I rejoiced over the birth of your son Seth. But after a little while I sorrowed greatly over Eve, because she is my sister. For when God sent a deep sleep over you, and drew her out of your side, He brought me out with her. But He raised her by placing her with you, while He lowered me.

10 "I rejoiced over my sister for her being with you. But God had

made me a promise before, and said, 'Do not grieve; when Adam has gone up on the roof of the Cave of Treasures, and is separated from Eve his wife, I will send you to him and you shall join yourself to him in marriage, and bear five children for him, as Eve gave him five children.'

11 "And now, look! God's promise to me is fulfilled because it is He who has sent me to you for the wedding, because if you wed me I shall bear you finer and better children than those of Eve.

12 "You are still young. Do not end your youth in this world in sorrow. Spend the days of your youth in happiness and pleasure. Your days are few and your trials have been great. Be strong and end your days in this world in rejoicing. I shall take pleasure in you, and you shall rejoice with me in this way and without fear.

13 "Get up and fulfill the command of your God," she then came near Adam and embraced him.

14 But when Adam saw that he was going to be overcome by her, he prayed to God with a fervent heart to deliver him from her.

15 Then God sent His Word to Adam, saying, "Adam, that apparition is the one that promised you the Godhead, and majesty. He does not intend good for you, but shows himself to you at one time in the form of a woman and in another moment in the likeness of an angel, and on another occasions in the apparition of a serpent, and at another time in the semblance of a god. But he does all of this only to destroy your soul.

16 " Adam, now that you understand this in your heart you will see that I have delivered you many a time from his hands in order to

show you that I am a merciful God. I wish you good and I do not wish your ruin."

Chapter IV.

1 Then God ordered Satan to show himself to Adam in his own hideous form, plainly.

2 But when Adam saw him he feared and trembled at the sight of him.

3 And God said to Adam, 'Look at this devil, and at his hideous sight, and know that he it is who made you fall from brightness into darkness, from peace and rest to toil and misery.

4 And look at him, Adam. He is the one who said that he is God! Can God be black? Would God take the form of a woman? Is there any one stronger than God? And can He be overpowered?

5 "See Adam. Look at him bound in your presence, in the air, unable to flee away! So, I say to you, do not be afraid of him. From now on, take care, and beware of him. He will try to do things to you."

6 Then God drove Satan away from Adam. And God strengthened Adam's heart and comforted him, saying, "Go down to the Cave of Treasures, and do not separate yourself from Eve. I will quiet all of your animal lust."

7 From that hour it left Adam and Eve, and they enjoyed rest by the commandment of God. But God did not do the same to any of Adam's seed (relations). God did this only to Adam and Eve.

8 Then Adam worshipped before the Lord for delivering him, and for

having subdued his passions. And he came down from above the cave, and lived with Eve as had done before.

9 This ended the forty days of his separation from Eve.

Chapter V

1 When Seth was seven years old, he knew good and evil, and was consistent in fasting and praying, and spent all his nights in praying to God for mercy and forgiveness.

2 He also fasted when bringing up his offering every day. He fasted more than his father did because his demeanor was beautiful, like that of an angel of God. He also had a good heart, and his soul was precious; and for this reason he brought up his offering every day.

3 And God was pleased with his offering, but He was also pleased with his purity. And he continued doing the will of God, and of his father and mother until he was seven years old.

4 After that, as he was coming down from the altar after giving his offering, Satan appeared to him in the form of a beautiful angel, brilliant with light, with a staff of light in his hand, and wrapped with a girdle of light.

5 He greeted Seth with a beautiful smile, and began to beguile him with beautiful words, saying to him, "Seth, why do you live in this mountain? It is rough, full of stones and sand, and trees with no good fruit on them. It is a wilderness without houses or towns, no good place to live in. But everywhere there is heat, weariness, and trouble."

6 He said further, 'But we live in beautiful places, in a world other than this earth. Our world is one of light and we live in the best conditions. Our women are more beautiful than any others. Seth, I wish you to marry one of them, because I see that you are handsome to look at. In this land there is not one woman good enough for you and there are only five souls in it.

7 "But in our world there are many men and many young, unmarried women, all more beautiful one than the other. So, I wish to remove you from here so that you may see my relations and be wedded to which ever you like.

8 "You shall live by me and be at peace. You shall be filled with glory and light, just as we are.

9 "You shall remain in our world and rest from this world and its misery. You shall never again feel weak and weary. You shall never bring up an offering or appeal for mercy. You shall commit no more sin nor be swayed by passions.

10 "And if you will listen to what I say, you shall wed one of my daughters because to us it is not a sin and it is not considered animal lust.

11 "For in our world we have no God because we all are gods and we all are of the light and are heavenly, powerful, strong and glorious."

Chapter VI

1 When Seth heard these words he was amazed, and began to believe Satan's treacherous speech, and said to him, "You said there is

another world created other than this one, and there are other creatures more beautiful than the creatures that are in this world?"

2 And Satan said, "Yes; you have heard me correctly, and I will tell you more good things about them and their ways."

3 But Seth said to him, "Your words have amazed me, and your beautiful description of it all."

4 "But I cannot go with you today, at least not until I have gone to my father Adam and to my mother Eve, and told them all you have said to me. Then if they give me permission to go with you, I will come."

5 Seth said, "I am afraid of doing any thing without my father's and mother's permission. I do not want to perish like my brother Cain, and like my father Adam, who transgressed the commandment of God. But, you know your way to this place, so come and meet me here tomorrow."

6 When Satan heard this, he said to Seth, "If you tell your father Adam what I have told you, he will not let you come with me.

7 But listen to me, do not tell your father and mother what I have said to you. Instead, come with me today. Come now to our world where you will see beautiful things and enjoy yourself there, and celebrate this day among my children, watching them and taking your fill of happiness; and have joy there. Then I shall bring you back to this place tomorrow. However, if you would rather stay there with me, so be it."

8 Then Seth answered, "The hope / love (spirit) of my father and of my mother, hangs on me and if I hide from them one day, they will die, and God will hold me guilty of sinning against them.

9 "And if they know that I have come to this place they assume it is to bring up my offering, and they would expect not to be separated from me one hour. Neither should I go to any other place unless they let me. But they treat me most kindly, because I always come back to them quickly."

10 Then Satan said to him, "What will happen to you if you were to disappear from them one night, and return to them at break of day?"

(Author's note: The assumption here is that he would sneak out after they fell asleep and not tell them.)

11 But Seth, when he saw how he kept on talking, and that he would not leave him alone, he ran and went up to the altar, and spread his hands to God, and sought deliverance from God.

12 Then God sent His Word, and cursed Satan, who fled from Him.

13 But Seth had gone up to the altar, saying in his heart. "The altar is the place of offering, and God is there. A divine fire shall consume what is on it and so Satan will be unable to hurt me, and shall not take me away from here."

14 Then Seth came down from the altar and went to his father and mother, whom he found on his way and who were longing to hear his voice, because he had been missing a while.

15 He then began to tell them what had befallen him from Satan, under the form of an angel.

16 But when Adam heard his account, he kissed his face, and warned him against that angel, telling him it was Satan who appeared to him.

Then Adam took Seth, and they went to the Cave of Treasures and rejoiced there.

17 But from that day on Adam and Eve were never separated from him wherever he went, whether for his offering or for any thing else.

18 This sign happened to Seth, when he was nine years old.

Chapter VII.

1 When our father Adam saw that Seth was of a perfect heart, he wished him to marry; lest the enemy should appear to him another time, and overcome him.

2 So Adam said to his son Seth, "I wish, 0 my son, that you wed your sister Aklia, Abel's sister, that she may bear you children, who shall replenish the earth, according to God's promise to us.

3 "Be not afraid, my son; there is no disgrace in it. I wish you to marry, from fear that if you do not the enemy could overcome you.'

4 Seth, however, did not wish to marry; but in obedience to his father and mother, he did not say a word.

5 So Adam married him to Aklia. And he was fifteen years old.

6 But when he was twenty years of age, he had a son, whom he called Enos (Enoch); and then had other children.

7 Then Enos grew up, married, and begat Cainan.

8 Cainan also grew up, married, and begat Mahalaleel.

9 Those fathers were born during Adam's lifetime, and dwelt by the Cave of Treasures.

10 Then were the days of Adam nine hundred and thirty years, and

those of Mahalaleel one hundred. But Mahalaleel, when he was grown up, loved fasting, praying, and with hard work, until the end of our father Adam's days drew near.

Chapter VIII.

1 When our father Adam saw that his end was near, he called his son Seth, who came to him in the Cave of Treasures, and he said to him: 2 "Seth, my son, bring me your children and your children's children, so that I may shed my blessing on them before I die." 3 When Seth heard these words from his father Adam, he went from him, shed a flood of tears over his face, and gathered together his children and his children's children, and brought them to his father Adam. 4 But when our father Adam saw them around him, he wept at having to be separated from them. 5 And when they saw him weeping, they all wept together, and kissed his face saying, "How shall you be separated from us, father? And how shall the earth receive you and hide you from our eyes?" Thus they lamented with words like these. 6 Then our father Adam blessed them all, and said to Seth, after he had blessed them: 7 "Seth, my son, you know this world and that it is full of sorrow, and of weariness; and you know all that has come upon us from our trials in it. So, I command you in these words: I want you to keep being innocent, to be pure and just, and trusting in God; and do not

believe the words of Satan, nor the apparitions in which he will show himself to you.

8 But keep the commandments that I give you this day; then give the same to your son Enos; and let Enos give it to his son Cainan; and Cainan to his son Mahalaleel; so that this commandment abide firm among all your children.

9 "Seth, my son, the moment I am dead take you my body and wrap it up with myrrh, aloes, and cassia, and leave me here in this Cave of Treasures in which are all the tokens which God gave us from the garden.

10 "My son, after a while a flood will come and overwhelm all creatures, and leave only eight souls out of it.

11 "But, my son, let those whom it will leave from among your children at that time, take my body with them out of this cave; and when they have taken it with them, let the oldest among them command his children to lay my body in a ship until the flood recedes, and they come out of the ship.

12 Then they shall take my body and lay it in the middle of the earth, shortly after they have been saved from the waters of the flood.

13 "The place where my body shall be laid is the middle of the earth and God shall come from that place and shall save all our kindred.

14 "But now, Seth, my son, place yourself at the head of your people. Tend to them and watch over them in the fear of God. Lead them in the good way. Command them to fast to God, and make them understand they should not to listen to Satan, or he will destroy them.

15 "I tell you again, separate your children and your children's children from Cain's children. Do not let them ever mix with them, nor come near them either to talk or to work."

16 Then Adam let his blessing descend upon Seth, and upon his children, and upon all his children's children.

17 He then turned to his son Seth, and to Eve his wife, and, said to them, "Preserve this gold, this incense, and this myrrh, that God has given us for a sign, because in days that are coming a flood will overwhelm the whole creation. But those who shall go into the ark shall take with them the gold, the incense, and the myrrh, together with my body, and will lay the gold, the incense, and the myrrh, with my body in the middle of the earth.

18 "Then, after a long time, the city in which the gold, the incense, and the myrrh are found with my body, shall be plundered. But when it is spoiled, the gold the incense, and the myrrh shall be taken care of with the spoil that is kept; and none of them shall perish, until the made man from the Word of God shall come. And kings shall take them, and shall offer to Him, gold in token of His being King; incense, in token of His being God of heaven and earth; and myrrh, in token of His passion.

19 "Gold also, as a token of His overcoming Satan, and all our foes; incense as a token that He will rise from the dead, and be exalted above things in heaven and things in the earth; and myrrh, in token that He will drink bitter gall; and feel the pains of hell from Satan.

20 "And now, Seth, my son, I have revealed to you hidden mysteries, which God had revealed to me. Keep my commandment for yourself

and for your people."

Chapter IX

1 When Adam had ended his commandment to Seth, his limbs went limp, his hands and feet lost all strength, his voice became silent, and his tongue ceased to speak. He closed his eyes and gave up the ghost.
2 But when his children saw that he was dead, they threw themselves over him, men and women, old and young, weeping.
3 The death of Adam took place at the end of nine hundred and thirty years that he lived upon the earth; on the fifteenth day of Barmudeh, after the reckoning of an epact of the sun, at the ninth hour.

(Author's note: Barmudeh is the third month of the Egyptian calendar. The epact is the number of days into the moon's cycle that the solar calendar begins. Thus, it is the difference in days between the solar and lunar calendar.) (Adam had to die before his 1000th birthday so that he would fulfill the death curse from God. 1000 years is as one day.)

4 It was on a Friday, the very day on which he was created, and on which he rested. And the hour at which he died was the same as that at which he came out of the garden.
5 Then Seth wrapped him up well, and embalmed him with plenty of sweet spices, from sacred trees and from the Holy Mountain. And he laid his body on the eastern side of the inside of the cave, the side of

the incense; and placed a lamp stand in front of him that kept burning.

6 Then his children stood before him weeping and wailing over him the entire night, until break of day.

7 Then Seth and his son Enos (Enoch), and Cainan, the son of Enos, went out and took good offerings to present to the Lord, and they came to the altar upon which Adam offered gifts to God.

8 But Eve said to them, "Wait until we have first asked God to accept our offering, and to keep the soul of Adam His servant by Him, and to take it up to rest."

9 And they all stood up and prayed.

Chapter X.

1 And when they had ended their prayer the Word of God came and comforted them concerning their father Adam.

2 After this, they offered their gifts for themselves and for their father.

3 And when they had ended their offering, the Word of God came to Seth, the eldest among them, saying to him, "Seth, Seth, Seth, three times. As I was with your father, so also shall I be with you, until the fulfillment of the promise I made your father saying, I will send My Word and save you and your seed.

4 "But as to your father Adam, keep you the commandment he gave you; and protect your seed (offspring) and keep them from that of Cain your brother."

5 And God withdrew His Word from Seth.

6 Then Seth, Eve, and their children, came down from the mountain to the Cave of Treasures.

7 But Adam was the first whose soul died in the land of Eden, in the Cave of Treasures; for no one died before him, but his son Abel, who died because he was murdered.

8 Then all the children of Adam rose up, and wept over their father Adam, and made offerings to him, one hundred and forty days.

Chapter XI.

1 After the death of Adam and of Eve, Seth separated his children, and his children's children, from Cain's children. Cain and his seed went down and lived to the west, below the place where he had killed his brother Abel.

2 But Seth and his children, lived to the north on the mountain of the Cave of Treasures, in order to be near to their father Adam.

3 And Seth the oldest (of his people), tall and good, with a worthy soul, and of a strong mind, stood at the head of his people; and tended to them in innocence, patience, and meekness, and did not allow even one of them to go down to Cain's children.

4 And because of their purity, they were named "Children of God," and they were with God instead of the hosts of angels who fell, for they continued in praises to God and in singing songs to Him in their cave, the Cave of Treasures.

5 Then Seth stood before the bodies of his father Adam and of his

mother Eve, and he prayed night and day and asked for mercy for himself and his children, and that when he had some difficulty dealing with a child, God would give him counsel.

6 But Seth and his children did not like mundane work, but set themselves to do heavenly things, because they had no other thought other than praises, worship, and psalms to God.

7 Therefore did they at all times hear the voices of angels, praising and glorifying God; from within the garden, or when they were sent by God on an errand, or when they were going up to heaven.

8 Because of their own purity, Seth and his children heard and saw the angels. The garden was not far above them, only about fifteen spiritual (heavenly) cubits.

9 One spiritual cubit is equal to three cubits of man, altogether forty-five cubits.

10 Seth and his children lived on the mountain below the garden. They did not sow nor reap. They made no food for the body, not even wheat, but only enough for offerings. They ate the flavorful fruit of trees that grew on the mountain where they lived.

11 Seth often fasted for forty days, as did also his oldest children. The family of Seth smelled the smell of the trees in the garden when the wind blew that way.

12 They were happy, innocent, without sudden fear, there was no jealousy, no evil action, nor hatred among them. There was no animal passion. No one among them spoke either foul words or curse. There was neither evil intention nor fraud. The men of that time never swore, but when under hard circumstances, when men

must swear, they swore by the blood of Abel the just.

13 But every day they compelled their children and their women to fast and pray, and to worship the most High God, in the cave. They blessed themselves by being near the body of their father Adam, and anointed themselves (with it).

14 And they did so until the end of Seth drew near.

(Author's note: It is unclear what the men anointed themselves with. It could be oil blessed by being left close to the body of Adam. To think that they anointed themselves with the oils from the dead body would violate religious laws that would be established latter than the story, yet far earlier than the writing of this 3rd century text.)

Chapter XII

1 Then Seth, the just, called his son Enos, and Cainan, the son of Enos, and Mahalaleel, the son of Cainan, and said he to them:

2 "My end is near, and I wish to build a roof over the altar on which gifts are offered."

3 They listened to his commandment and all of them, both old and young, went out and worked hard and built a beautiful roof over the altar.

4 And Seth's thought was that by doing this a blessing should come upon his children on the mountain. And he though he should present an offering for them before his death.

5 Then when the building of the roof was completed, he commanded

them to make offerings. They worked diligently and brought them to Seth, their father, who took them and offered them upon the altar, and prayed God to accept their offerings, to have mercy on the souls of his children, and to keep them from the hand of Satan.

6 God accepted his offering and sent His blessing on him and on his children. Then God made a promise to Seth, saying, "At the end of the great five days and a half, which is the promise I have made to you and to your father, I will send My Word and save you and your seed." *(Author's note: A great day is 1000 years.)*

7 Then Seth and his children, and grandchildren met together and came down from the altar and went to the Cave of Treasures, where they prayed. And he blessed them in the body of our father Adam, and anointed them with it.

8 But Seth stayed in the Cave of Treasures, a few days, and then suffered - sufferings to death.

9 Then Enos, his first born son, came to him with Cainan, his son, and Mahalaleel, Cainan's son, and Jared, the son of Mahalaleel, and Enoch, Jared's son, and with their wives and children to receive a blessing from Seth.

10 Then Seth prayed over them, and blessed them, and earnestly requested them by the blood of Abel the just, saying, "I beg of you my children, not to let one of you go down from this Holy and pure Mountain.

11 Do not associate with the children of Cain the murderer and the sinner, who killed his brother. You know, my children, that we flee from him and from all his sin with all our might because he killed his

brother Abel."

12 After having said this, Seth blessed Enos, his first-born son, and commanded him to minister continually in purity before the body of their father Adam, all the days of his life. He also made him promise to go at times to the altar, which he had built. And he commanded him to feed his people in righteousness, in judgment, and in purity all the days of his life.

13 Then Seth's limbs went limp. His hands and feet lost all strength. His voice became silent and unable to speak, and he gave up the ghost and died. Seth died the day after his nine hundred and twelfth year, on the twenty - seventh day of the month Abib; Enoch being then twenty years old.

(Author's note: There are three separate numbers of significance here. 27 is a gateway number to 9. 2+7=9. Nine is the number of endings. 912 reduces to the number 3, which is number of completeness. Abib is the seventh month of the year in the Hebrew calendar, corresponding to Nisan.)

14 Then they carefully wrapped up the body of Seth, and embalmed him with sweet spices, and laid him in the Cave Treasures, on the right side of our father Adam's body, and they mourned for him forty days. They offered gifts for him, as they had done for our father Adam.

15 After the death of Seth, Enos was raised to the head of his people, whom he fed in righteousness, and judgment, as his father had commanded him.

16 But by the time Enos was eight hundred and twenty years old, Cain had a very large number of offspring, because they had sex (married) often, being given to animal lusts, until the land below the mountain, was filled with them.

Chapter XIII

1 Lamech the blind lived in those days. He was one of the sons of Cain. He had a son whose name was Atun, and the two of them had many cattle.

2 Lamech was in the habit of sending them to graze with a young shepherd, who tended them. He was coming home in the evening when he went to his grandfather, his father Atun, and his mother Hazina, and he wept and he said to them, " I cannot feed those cattle alone, or someone may rob me of some of them, or kill me so they can take them." Because among the children of Cain there was a lot of robbery, murder, and sin.

3 Then Lamech pitied him, and he said, "You may be correct. When you are alone you might be overpowered by the men of this place."

4 So Lamech arose, took a bow he had kept ever since he was a youth, before he became blind, and he took large arrows, and smooth stones, and a sling, which he had, and he went to the field with the young shepherd, and placed himself behind the cattle while the young shepherd watched the cattle. Lamech did this for many days.

5 Meanwhile, ever since God had cast him off and had cursed him

with trembling and fear, Cain could not be still (settle) nor find rest in any one place, so he wandered from place to place.

6 In his wanderings he came to Lamech's wives, and asked them about him. They said to him, "He is in the field with the cattle."

7 Then Cain went to look for him and as he came into the field, the young shepherd heard the noise he made, and the cattle herding together in front of him.

8 Then said he to Lamech, "My lord, is that a wild beast or a robber?"

9 And Lamech said to him, "Tell me where he is when he comes up."

10 Then Lamech bent his bow, placed an arrow on it, and fitted a stone in the sling, and when Cain came out from the open country, the shepherd said to Lamech, "Shoot, behold, he is coming."

11 Then Lamech shot at Cain with his arrow and hit him in his side. And Lamech struck him with a stone from his sling, and the stone struck his face and knocked out both his eyes. Then Cain fell dead instantly.

12 Then Lamech and the young shepherd came up to him and found him lying on the ground. And the young shepherd said to him, "It is Cain our grandfather, whom you have killed, my lord!"

18 Then Lamech grieved in bitterness and regret. And he clapped his hands together and struck the head of the youth with his flat palm, and the youth fell as if he were dead. But Lamech thought the youth was pretending, so he took up a stone and struck him, and smashed his head until he died.

Chapter XIV

1 When Enos was nine hundred years old, all the children of Seth, and of Cainan, and his first-born, with their wives and children, gathered around him, asking for a blessing from him.

2 Then he prayed over them and blessed them, and made them promise them by the blood of Abel the just, saying to them, "Do not let even one of your children go down from this Holy Mountain, and do not let them make friends with the children of Cain the murderer."

3 Then Enos called his son Cainan and said to him, "Look, my son, and set your heart on your people, and establish them in righteousness, and in innocence, and stand ministering before the body of our father Adam, all the days of your life."

4 After this Enos rested (died). He was nine hundred and eighty - five years old. Cainan wrapped him up, and laid him in the Cave of Treasures on the left of his father Adam, and made offerings for him, following the custom of his fathers.

Chapter XV

1 After the death of Enos, Cainan led his people in righteousness and innocence, as his father had commanded him. He also continued to minister before the body of Adam, in the Cave of Treasures.

2 Then when he had lived nine hundred and ten years, suffering and sickness came upon him. And when he was about to enter into rest

(die), all the fathers with their wives and children came to him, and he blessed them, and earnestly urged them by the blood of Abel, the just, saying to them, "Let no one among you descend from this Holy Mountain; and do not make friends with the children of Cain the murderer."

3 Mahalaleel, his first - born son, received this commandment from his father, who blessed him and died.

4 Then Mahalaleel embalmed him with sweet spices, and laid him in the Cave of Treasures, with his fathers; and they made offerings for him, as was the custom of their fathers.

Chapter XVI

1 Then Mahalaleel led his people, and fed them in righteousness and innocence, and watched them to see they had no relationship with the children of Cain.

2 He also continued in the Cave of Treasures praying and ministering before the body of their father Adam, asking God for mercy on himself and on his people, until he was eight hundred and seventy years old, when he fell sick.

3 Then all his children gathered around him to see him, and to ask for his blessing on them all, before he left this world.

4 Then Mahalaleel arose and sat on his bed, his tears streaming down his face, and he called his eldest son Jared, who came to him.

5 He then kissed his face, and said to him, "Jared, my son, I solemnly urge you by Him who made heaven and earth, to watch over your

people, and to feed them in righteousness and in innocence; and not to let even one of them go down from this Holy Mountain to the children of Cain, or he will perish with them.

6 "Hear, my son, there will come a great destruction upon this earth because of them. God will be angry with the world, and will destroy them with waters.

7 "But I also know that your children will not listen to you, and that they will go down from this mountain and have relations with the children of Cain, and that they shall perish with them.

8 " My son! Teach them, and watch over them, so that no guilt will be on you because of them."

9 Mahalaleel continued, saying to his son Jared, "When I die, embalm my body and lay it in the Cave of Treasures, by the bodies of my forefathers then stand by my body and pray to God, and take care of them, and fulfill your ministry before them, until you enter into rest yourself."

10 Mahalaleel then blessed all his children, then he laid down on his bed and entered into rest like his fathers.

11 But when Jared saw that his father Mahalaleel was dead, he wept and grieved, and embraced, and kissed his hands and his feet, and so did all his children.

12 And his children embalmed him carefully, and laid him by the bodies of his fathers. Then they stood and mourned for him forty days.

(Author's note: Mahalaleel's way of adjuring Jared, his son, was different in

form from those before. He did not invoke the name of Abel, the just. The results were also different, in that it was at this time the children of Abel first began to have intercourse with the children of Cain.)

Chapter XVII

1 Then Jared kept his father's commandment, and arose like a lion over his people. He fed them in righteousness and innocence, and commanded them to do nothing without his consent. This was because he was afraid for them that they should go to the children of Cain.

2 He gave them orders repeatedly, and continued to do so until the end of the four hundred and eighty-fifth year of his life.

3 At the end of these years, there came to him a sign. As Jared was standing like a lion before the bodies of his fathers, praying and warning his people, Satan envied him and produced a beautiful specter because Jared would not let his children do anything without his counsel.

4 Satan appeared to him with thirty men of his hosts, in the form of handsome men. Satan himself was the oldest and tallest among them, with a fine beard.

5 They stood at the mouth of the cave, and called out Jared, who was in the cave.

6 He came out to them and found them looking like handsome men, full of light, and very beautiful. He was in awe of their beauty and their looks, and wondered to himself whether they might not be of

the children of Cain.

7 He said also in his heart, " The children of Cain cannot come up to the height of this mountain, and none of them are this handsome as these appear to be, and among these men there is not one of my kindred, so they must be strangers."

8 Then Jared exchanged a greeting with them and he said to the oldest among them, " My father, tell me how you are so wonderful, and tell me who these are with you. They look to me like strange men."

9 Then the oldest began to weep and the rest wept with him, and he said to Jared, "I am Adam whom God made first, and this is Abel my son, who was killed by his brother Cain, whose heart was influenced by Satan to murder.

10 "And this is my son Seth, whom I asked Lord to give me to comfort me when I no longer had Abel.

11 "Then this one is my son Enos, son of Seth, and that other one is Cainan, son of Enos, and that other one is Mahalaleel, son of Cainan, your father."

12 But Jared remained wondering at their appearance and at the words of the elder to him.

13 Then the oldest said to him, "Do not stand there is awe, my son. We now live in the land north of the garden, which God created before the world. He would not let us live there, but placed us inside the garden, below which you are now living.

14 "After I transgressed, He made me come out of it and I was left to live in this cave. That was when great and horrible troubles came on

me. And when the time of my death drew near, I commanded my son Seth to tend his people well. And my commandment is to be handed from one to another, to the end of the generations to come.

15 "But, Jared, my son, we live in beautiful regions while you live here in misery. Your father Mahalaleel informed me that a great flood would come and overwhelm the whole earth.

16 "Therefore, my son, fearing for your sakes, I rose and took my children with me, and came here to visit you and your children. I found you standing in this cave weeping, and your children scattered about this mountain in the heat and in misery.

17 "But, my son, as we missed our way, and came as far as this, we found other men below this mountain; who inhabit a beautiful country, full of trees and of fruits, and of all manner of lush, green vegetation. It is like a garden. When we found them we thought they were you, until your father Mahalaleel told me they were no such thing.

18 "Now, my son, listen to my advice, and go down to them, you and your children. You will rest from all this suffering you are in. If you will not go down to them then arise, take your children, and come with us to our garden. There, you shall live in our beautiful land, and you shall rest from all this trouble which you and your children are now living in."

19 But when he heard these words from the oldest, Jared was confused and went here and there, but at that moment he found none of his children.

20 Then he answered and said to the old one, "Why have you hidden

yourselves until this day?"

21 And the oldest replied, "If your father had not told us, we would not have known it."

22 Then Jared believed his words were true.

23 So that oldest said to Jared, "Wherefore did you turn about, so and so?" And he said, "I was seeking one of my children, to tell him about my going with you, and about their coming down to those about whom you have spoken to me."

24 When the old one heard Jared's intention, he said to him, "Do not worry about that right now but come with us and you shall see our country. If the land in which we live pleases you, we shall all return here and take your family with us. But if our country does not please you, you shall come back to your own home."

25 And the old one urged Jared to go before one of his children came to talk him out of his decision.

26 Jared, then, came out of the cave and went with them, and among them. And they comforted him, until they came to the top of the mountain of the sons of Cain.

27 Then the old one said to one of his companions, "We have forgotten something by the mouth of the cave, and that is the chosen garment we had brought to clothe Jared with."

28 He then said to one of them, "One of you go back, and we will wait for you here until you come back. Then will we clothe Jared and he shall be like us, good, handsome, and fit to come with us into our country."

29 Then that one went back.

30 But when he was a short distance off, the old one called to him and said to him, "You stay there until I come up and speak to you." 31 Then he stood still and the old one went up to him and said to him, "One thing we forgot at the cave, it is this; we forgot to put out the lamp that burns inside the cave, above the bodies that are in there. Do it and come back to us, quickly."

32 That one went, and the old one came back to his fellows and to Jared. And they came down from the mountain, and Jared was with them. And they stayed by a fountain of water, near the houses of the children of Cain and waited for their companion until he brought the garment for Jared.

33 Then he who went back to the cave, put out the lamp, and came to them and brought an apparition with him and showed it them. And when Jared saw it he wondered at the beauty and grace thereof, and rejoiced in his heart believing it was all true.

34 But while they were staying there, three of them went into houses of the sons of Cain and said to them, "Bring us today some food by the fountain of water, for us and our companions to eat."

35 But when the sons of Cain saw them, they were in awe at them and thought: "These men are beautiful to look at. We have never seen such before." So they rose and came with them to the fountain of water, to see their companions.

36 They thought them so very handsome that they called aloud about their places for others to gather together and come and look at these beautiful beings. Then they gathered around them both men and women.

37 Then the old one said to them, "We are strangers in your land, bring us some good food and drink, and bring yourselves and your women, so we can entertain (refresh) ourselves with you."

38 When those men heard these words of the old one, every one of Cain's sons brought his wife, and another brought his daughter, and so, many women came to them; every one calling out to Jared either for himself or for his wife.

39 But when Jared saw what they did, his very soul wrenched itself from them and he would not taste their food or their drink.

40 The old one saw him as he wrenched himself from them, and said to him, "Do not be sad. I am the great elder, as you shall see me do, do yourself in like manner."

41 Then he spread his hands and took one of the women, and five of his companions did the same in front of Jared, that he should do as they did.

42 But when Jared saw them doing their wickedness he wept, and said in his mind, "My fathers never acted like this."

43 He then spread his hands and prayed with a fervent heart, and with much weeping, and begged God to deliver him from their hands.

44 No sooner did Jared begin to pray than the old one fled with his companions; for they could not abide in a place of prayer.

45 Then Jared turned round but could not see them, but found himself standing in the midst of the children of Cain.

46 He then wept and said, "0 God, do not destroy me with this race, concerning which my fathers have warned me. For now, my Lord

God, I was thinking that those who appeared to me were my
forefathers, but I have found them out to be devils, who lured me by
way of this beautiful apparition, until I believed them.

47 "But now I ask You, 0 God, to deliver me from this race, among
whom I am now staying, as You did deliver me from those devils.
Send Your angel to pull me out of the middle of them. I do not have
the power within myself to escape from among them."

48 When Jared had ended his prayer, God sent His angel into the
middle of them and he took Jared and set him up on the mountain,
and showed him the way, and he gave him wise advice, and then
departed from him.

Chapter XVIII

1 The children of Jared were in the habit of visiting him hour after
hour, to receive his blessing and to ask his advice for every thing
they did, and when he had work to do, they did it for him.

2 But this time when they went into the cave they did not find Jared,
but they found the lamp put out, and the bodies of the fathers
thrown about, and voices came from them by the power of God, that
said, "Satan in an apparition has deceived our son, wishing to
destroy him, as he destroyed our son Cain."

3 They said also, "Lord God of heaven and earth, deliver our son
from the hand of Satan, who produced such a great and false specter
before him." They also spoke of other matters, by the power of God.

4 But when the children of Jared heard these voices they feared, and

stood weeping for their father because they did not know what had happened to him.

5 And they wept for him that day until the setting of the sun.

6 Then Jared come with a mournful expression, miserable in mind and body, and sorrowful at having been separated from the bodies of his fathers.

7 But as he came near the cave, his children saw him and ran to the cave, and hugged his neck, crying, and saying to him, "0 father, where have you been, and why have you left us because we know you did not want to?" And they spoke again saying, "Father, when you disappeared the lamp over the bodies of our fathers went out, and the bodies were thrown about, and voices came from them"

8 When Jared heard this he was sorry, and went into the cave; and there found the bodies thrown about, the lamp put out, and the fathers themselves praying for his deliverance from the hand of Satan.

9 Then Jared fell upon the bodies and embraced them, and said, "My fathers, through your intercession, God delivered me from the hand of Satan! I beg you to ask God to keep me and to hide me from him to the day of my death."

10 Then all the voices ceased except the voice of our father Adam, who spoke to Jared by the power of God, just as one would speak to his friend, saying, "Jared, my son, offer gifts to God for having delivered you from the hand of Satan. And when you bring those offerings, offer them on the same altar on which I gave offerings. Even then you must beware of Satan, for he deluded me many a time

with his specters, wishing to destroy me, but God delivered me out of his hand.

11 "Command your people that they be on their guard against him, and never cease to offer up gifts to God."

12 Then the voice of Adam also became silent; and Jared and his children wondered at this. Then they laid the bodies as they were at first; and Jared and his children stood praying the entire night, until break of day.

13 Then Jared made an offering and offered it up on the altar, as Adam had commanded him. And as he went up to the altar, he prayed to God for mercy and for forgiveness of his sin concerning the lamp going out.

14 Then God appeared to Jared on the altar and blessed him and his children, and accepted their offerings; and commanded Jared to take of the sacred fire from the altar and light the lamp that shed light on the body of Adam.

Chapter XIX

1 Then God again revealed to him the promise He had made to Adam. He explained to him the 5500 years, and revealed to him the mystery of His coming to the earth.

2 And God said to Jared, "Let that fire you have taken from the altar to light the lamp abide with you to give light to the bodies. Do not let it come out of the cave until the body of Adam comes out.

3 But, Jared, take care of the fire, so that it burns brightly in the lamp.

Do not go out of the cave again until you received an order through a vision, and not in an apparition, you see.

(Author's note: The distinction here is that a vision is internal and an apparition is external. Only God can guide us internally. Satan must entice and trick through external ploys.)

4 "Then command your people again not to have relations with the children of Cain, and not to learn their ways, for I am God who does not love hatred and works of iniquity."

5 God also gave many other commandments to Jared, and He blessed him. And then withdrew His Word from him.

6 Then Jared came near to his children, took some fire, and came down to the cave and lighted the lamp in front of the body of Adam. Then he gave his people the commandments just as God had told him to do.

7 This sign happened to Jared at the end of his four hundred and fiftieth year, as did many other wonders we did not record. But we record only this one for the sake of brevity to shorten our written account.

8 And Jared continued to teach his children eighty years, but after that they began to break the commandments he had given them, and to do many things without his permission. They began to go down from the Holy Mountain, one after another, and mix with the children of Cain, in obscene association.

9 Now the reason the children of Jared went down the Holy

Mountain will now be revealed to you.

Chapter XX.

1 After Cain had gone down to the land of dark soil, and his children had multiplied, there was one of them, whose name was Genun, son of Lamech the blind who slew Cain.

2 Satan came to Genun in his childhood and made a variety trumpets and horns, and string instruments, cymbals and psalteries, and lyres and harps, and flutes. And Genun played them at all times and at every hour.

3 And when he played them, Satan came to them so that from among them were heard beautiful and sweet sounds that seized the heart with delight.

4 Then he gathered many crowds to play on them, and when they played it greatly pleased the children of Cain, who fanned themselves to flames of sin among themselves and they burned with fire while Satan inflamed their hearts with one another, and lust increased among them.

5 Satan also taught Genun to make strong drink out of corn. Genun used this to bring together crowd upon crowd in houses of drink, and brought into their hands all kinds of fruits and flowers, and they drank together.

6 Genun did this to multiply sin greatly. He also acted with pride, and taught the children of Cain to commit all manner of the grossest wickedness, which they did not know until then. And he put them

up to all kinds of deeds, which they did not know of before.

7 Then, when Satan saw that they obeyed Genun and listened to him in every thing he told them, he rejoiced greatly, and he increased Genun's understanding until he took iron and with it made weapons of war.

8 Then when they were drunk, hatred and murder increased among them. One man would use violence against another and Satan would teach him evil in that one man would take the other man's children and defile them before him.

9 And when men saw they were vanquished and saw that others were not beaten, those who were beaten came to Genun and took refuge with him, and he made them part of his group.

10 Then sin increased among them greatly, until a man married his own sister, or daughter, or mother, and others, or the daughter of his father's sister (first cousin), so that there was no more distinction of relationship, and they could no longer discern what was sin and what was not, but always were wicked and the earth was defiled with sin. And they angered God the Judge, who had created them.

11 But Genun gathered together groups and groups, that played on horns and on all the other instruments we have already mentioned, at the foot of the Holy Mountain. They did that so the children of Seth who were on the Holy Mountain would hear it.

12 But when the children of Seth heard the noise, they wondered, and came by companies, and stood on the top of the mountain to look at those below. This went on an entire year.

13 At the end of that year, Genun saw that they were being won over

to him little by little. Satan entered into him, and taught him to make the elements for dyeing garments of various patterns, and made him understand how to dye crimson and purple and what not.

14 And the sons of Cain who worked at all of this shone in beauty and gorgeous apparel. And they gathered together at the foot of the mountain in splendor, with horns and gorgeous dresses, and horse races, and they were committing all manner of disgusting acts.

15 Meanwhile the children of Seth, who were on the Holy Mountain, prayed and praised God in the place of the hosts of angels who had fallen. God had called them 'angels," because He rejoiced over them greatly.

16 But after this time they no longer kept His commandment, nor were held by the promise He had made to their fathers. But they relaxed from their fasting and praying, and from the counsel of Jared their father. And they kept on gathering together on the top of the mountain to watch the children of Cain, from morning until evening. And they watched what they did and they looked at their beautiful dresses and ornaments.

17 Then the children of Cain looked up from below, and saw the children of Seth, standing in numbers on the top of the mountain, and they called to them to come down to them.

18 But from above them, the children of Seth said, "We don't know the way." Then Genun, the son of Lamech, heard them say they did not know the way, and he began to think to himself of ways he might bring them down.

19 Then Satan appeared to him by night, saying, "There is no way for

them to come down from the part of the mountain on which they live, but when they come out tomorrow (to watch), say to them, 'Come to the western side of the mountain. There you will find a stream of water that comes down to the foot of the mountain, between two hills. That marks the way. Come down that way to us.'"

20 Then when it was day, Genun blew the horns and beat the drums below the mountain, as he was accustomed to do. The children of Seth heard it and came as they used to do.

21 Then Genun said to them from down below, "Go to the western side of the mountain, there you will find the way to come down."

22 But when the children of Seth heard these words from him, they went back into the cave to Jared to tell him all they had heard.

23 Then when Jared heard it, he was grieved because he knew that they would defy his wishes.

24 After this a hundred men of the children of Seth gathered together and said among themselves, "Come, let us go down to the children of Cain and see what they do, and enjoy ourselves with them."

25 But when Jared heard this of the hundred men his very soul was moved, and his heart was grieved. He then stood with great emotion in the middle of them, and earnestly compelled them by the blood of Abel the just and said, "Let no one of you go down from this holy and pure mountain, in which our fathers have ordered us to live."

26 But when Jared saw that they did not listen to his words, he said to them, "My good, innocent, and holy children, you must understand that once you go down from this holy mountain, God will not allow you to return to it again."

27 He again adjured them, saying, "I plead with you by the death of our father Adam, and by the blood of Abel, of Seth, of Enos, of Cainan, and of Mahalaleel, to listen to me. Do not go down from this holy mountain, because the moment you leave it, life and mercy will be taken from you; and you shall no longer be called 'children of God,' but 'children of the devil.'

28 But they would not listen to his words.

29 Enoch was already grown up at that time, and in his zeal for God, he stood and said, "Hear me, you large and small (young and old) sons of Seth! When you transgress the commandment of our fathers and go down from this holy mountain, you shall not come up here again for ever."

30 But they rose up against Enoch and would not listen to his words, but they went down from the Holy Mountain.

31 And when they looked at the daughters of Cain, at their beautiful figures, and at their hands and feet dyed with color, and the tattoos on their faces that ornamented them, the fire of sin was set ablaze in them.

32 Then Satan made them look most beautiful before the sons of Seth, as he also made the sons of Seth appear the most handsome in the eyes of the daughters of Cain, so that the daughters of Cain lusted after the sons of Seth like ravenous beasts, and the sons of Seth lusted after the daughters of Cain until they committed disgusting and disgraceful acts with them.

33 But after they had fallen into this defilement they returned by the way they had come, and tried to ascend the Holy Mountain. But they

could not because the stones of that holy mountain were on fire flashing before them, and prevented them so that they could not go up again.

34 And God was angry with them, and turned from them because they had come down from glory, and because of this had lost and forsaken their own purity and innocence, and were fallen into the defilement of sin.

35 Then God sent His Word to Jared, saying, "These of your children, whom you once called 'My children,' have broken My commandment, and have gone down to the house of damnation and sin. Send a messenger to those that are left so that they will not go down, and be lost."

36 Then Jared wept before the Lord, and asked Him for mercy and forgiveness. But he wished that his soul might depart from his body rather than hear these words from God about his children that went down from the Holy Mountain.

37 But he followed God's order and preached to them not to go down from that holy mountain, and not to hold relations with the children of Cain.

38 But they did not listen to his message, and they would not obey his advice.

Chapter XXI

1 After this, another group gathered together and went to look after their brothers but they perished with them as well. And so it was,

company after company, until only a few of them remained.

2 Then Jared was sickened with grief. And his sickness was such that the day of his death was near.

3 Then he called Enoch his eldest son, and Methuselah Enoch's son, and Lamech the son of Methuselah, and Noah the son of Lamech.

4 And when they came to him he prayed over them and blessed them, and said to them, "You are righteous, innocent sons. Do not go down from this holy mountain, because you have seen your children and your children's children have gone down from this holy mountain, and have alienated themselves from this holy mountain through their reprehensible lust and transgression of God's commandment.

5 But I know, through the power of God, that He will not leave you on this holy mountain. Your children have transgressed His commandment and that of our fathers, which we had received from them.

6 But, my sons, God will take you to a strange land, and you never shall return to see this garden and this holy mountain with your own eyes once again.

7 Therefore, my sons, set your hearts on your own selves, and keep the commandment of God which is with you. And when you go from this holy mountain into a strange land which you do not know, take the body of our father Adam with you, and with it take these three precious gifts and offerings, namely, the gold, the incense, and the myrrh; and let them be in the place where the body of our father Adam shall lay.

8 And, my sons, of you who are left, the Word of God will come, and when he goes out of this land he shall take with him the body of our father Adam, and shall lay it in the middle of the earth, the place in which salvation shall be worked out."

9 Then Noah said to him, "Who is he of us that shall be left?"

10 And Jared answered, "You are he that shall be left. And you shall take the body of our father Adam from the cave, and place it with you in the ark when the flood comes.

11 "And your son Shem, who shall come out of your loins, it is he who shall lay the body of our father Adam in the middle of the earth, in the place where salvation shall come."

12 Then Jared turned to his son Enoch, and said to him "My son, abide in this cave, and minister diligently before the body of our father Adam all the days of your life, and feed your people in righteousness and innocence."

13 And Jared said no more. His hands went limp, his eyes closed, and he entered into rest like his fathers. His death took place in the three hundred and sixtieth year of Noah, and in the nine hundred and eighty-ninth year of his own life; on the twelfth of Takhsas on a Friday.

(Author's note: In this year, the month of Takhsas was likely to be December.)

14 But as Jared died, tears streamed down his face by reason of his great sorrow, for the children of Seth, who had fallen in his days.

15 Then Enoch, Methuselah, Lamech and Noah, these four, wept over him; embalmed him carefully, and then laid him in the Cave of Treasures. Then they rose and mourned for him forty days.

16 And when these days of mourning were ended, Enoch, Methuselah, Lamech and Noah remained in sorrow of heart because their father had departed from them and could not see him again.

Chapter XXII

1 Enoch kept the commandment of Jared his father, and continued to minister in the cave.

2 Many wonders happened to this man, Enoch, and he also wrote a celebrated book; but those wonders may not be told in this place.

3 Then after this, the children of Seth, as well as their children and their wives went astray and fell. And when Enoch, Methuselah, Lamech and Noah saw them, their hearts suffered because of their fall, which filled them with doubt and unbelief. And they wept and sought of God mercy to preserve them, and to bring them out of that wicked generation.

4 Enoch continued in his ministry before the Lord three hundred and eighty-five years, and at the end of that time he became aware through the grace of God, that God intended to remove him from the earth.

5 He then said to his son, "0 my son, I know that God intends to bring the waters of the Flood on the earth, and destroy our (His) creation.

6 "And you are the last rulers over the people on this mountain. And

I know that not one (woman) will be left for you to have children on this holy mountain. Not one of you will rule over the children of his people. No great number of you will be left on this mountain."

7 Enoch also said to them, "Watch over your souls, and hold tight to your fear of God and your service to Him, and worship Him in righteous faith, and serve Him in righteousness, innocence and judgment. Worship Him in repentance and in purity."

8 When Enoch had ended his commandments to them, God transported him from that mountain to the land of life, to the mansions of the righteous and of the chosen ones, which is the abode of Paradise of joy, in light that reaches up to heaven. It is the light that is beyond the light of this world It is the light of God that fills the whole world and no place can contain.

9 Enoch was in the light of God and because of this he found himself out of the grasp of death, until God would have him die.

10 Altogether, not one of our fathers or of their children, remained on that holy mountain, except those three, Methuselah, Lamech, and Noah. All the rest went down from the mountain and fell into sin with the children of Cain. And they were forbidden to come back to that mountain. And none remained on it but those three men.

This completes The Second Book of Adam and Eve.

Author' Note:

In the preceding 171 pages we are confronted with the Genesis story, possibly embellished beyond recognition. Modern readers may find the story to be so fanciful as to be ridiculous. The story may appear to be repetitive and rife with storylines of Satanic deception and human frailty running in waves and cycles throughout the text. Yet, in this ancient script there is a central and universal question – and a singular answer.

How can we know if the circumstance, situation, or even the person in our life is an appointment of God or Satan?

If you are one of the millions of people who believe in an evil entity who is at war with God for the souls of mankind, this question is one of the most important of your life. It defines and clarifies if you are being obedient to God or being deceived by Satan.

Is it possible to know? According to the text, Satan has the power to produce apparitions, specters, and illusions, so believable that they cannot be distinguished from reality. Satan lies, and offers material enticements. Even these may be confused with the grace of God. After all, God gave Adam treasures to place in the cave for his comfort and consolation.

The answer to the eternal question is amazingly simple. Stop. Be still. Look within. Satan may be able to manipulate the material world, but he cannot touch the spirit. Satan may give apparitions and illusions, but God gives visions. The world is Satan's, but the soul is the domain of God. The mystical vision is the terrain of God to tread. Look there for the answer. He alone is there, waiting.

Made in the USA
Lexington, KY
03 January 2015

A gift from
Freida Isaac

Happy Birthday Jean! We hope that you enjoy your gift!
From: Henry and Family

A gift from
Freida Isaac

Enjoy your gift! From: Henry and Family

Returns Are Easy!Most items can be refunded, exchanged, or replaced when returned in original and unopened condition. Visit http://www.amazon.com/returns to start your return, or http://www.amazon.com/help for more information on return policies.

Have feedback on Amazon gifting? Tell us at www.amazon.com/giftingfeedback.

DMN47LbHk/-2 of 2-/second/9033843 UPS-LEXKY-T

Order ID 106-9451269-8276269 - Order of January 3, 2015

Qty.	Item
1	**The First and Second Books of Adam and Eve: The Conflict With Satan** Lumpkin, Dr. Joseph --- Paperback **(** 1-B-5 **)** 1933580526
1	**The Books of Enoch: The Angels, The Watchers and The Nephilim: (With Extensive Commentary on the Three Books of Enoch, t...** Lumpkin, Joseph --- Paperback **(** 1-B-5 **)** 1936533073

This completes your gift order.
Have feedback on how we packaged your order? Tell us at www.amazon.com/packaging.

34/DMN47LbHk/-2 of 2-//UPS-LEXKY-T/second/9033843/0105-15:00/0104-10:47